KARATE'S
History and Traditions

KARATE'S
History and Traditions

by Bruce A. Haines

CHARLES E. TUTTLE COMPANY
Rutland, Vermont & Tokyo, Japan

Representatives
Continental Europe: BOXERBOOKS, INC., *Zurich*
British Isles: PRENTICE-HALL INTERNATIONAL, INC., *London*
Australasia: PAUL FLESCH & CO., PTY. LTD., *Melbourne*
Canada: HURTIG PUBLISHERS, *Edmonton*

Published by the Charles E. Tuttle Company, Inc.
of Rutland, Vermont & Tokyo, Japan
with editorial offices at
Suido 1-chome, 2-6, Bunkyo-ku, Tokyo, Japan

Copyright in Japan, 1968 by Charles E. Tuttle Co., Inc.

Library of Congress Catalog Card No. 68-25893

International Standard Book No. 0-8048-0341-2

First edition, 1968
Eighth printing, 1974

PRINTED IN JAPAN

To
Dr. Minoru Shinoda

Table of Contents

List of Illustrations

Preface

MY INITIAL interest in karate started in 1954 as a student of the art in Honolulu. From that point thirteen years ago, through three karate schools, numerous instructors, and a master's thesis on karate history at the University of Hawaii, my attitude toward this fighting form has evolved from naive interest and dedication to a position of frustration and considerable hostility. Anger is not applicable to the detached and objectively oriented historian; however, anger has not been aimed at trying to prove one particular point or philosophy, but at enlightening America's monumental ignorance of karate per se, and its generally related arts.

To be more precise and to explain this irritation with concrete examples, I find the following to be particularly out of step with the philosophies of the progenitors of karate and its associated combat forms: karate tournaments whose referees and sponsors allow and often even encourage violence and mayhem in the "free-style" or *kumite* matches (something absolutely forbidden on Okinawa and in Japan) because of the added spectator appeal; instructors who give black belts (expert category) for mere hours of practice time spent, or for so-called business and/or political reasons; instructors whose main

concern is financial success and who thus charge out-
rageous fees, and who have infected the art with various
degrees of "questionable" contractual agreements for the
payment of same; individuals who involve themselves in
petty bickering over the question of who "deserves" to
head local, national, and international karate associations, each claiming superiority; those who boisterously
emphasize style or *ryu* superiority of one form over another; and lastly, those individuals with varying degrees
of karate knowledge who train with the secret hope that
someday they will have the opportunity to viciously test
their acquired "skills." This is but a partial list, though it
is sufficient to emphasize my point.

Karate as an ongoing sport and art is in such danger
of becoming Westernized (i.e., art for money's sake) that
it is hoped this work will enlighten *karate-ka* (karate practitioners) as to the philosophies, points-of-view, and hypotheses of those who have dedicated their lives to karate
in all of its ramifications through the centuries. If the
ensuing pages insult or trouble any individual, please be
certain that they are not intended to do so. History can
be written so antiseptically that personalities are all but
extinguished; this I have not done. But neither have I
attempted to make sensational accusations, name names,
become dogmatic beyond historical accuracy, or avoid
formulating hypotheses when the facts seemed to call for
such formulation. In fact, for those who feel the "brilliant light of truth bearing down unmercifully," it seems
appropriate to apply an old adage: "If the shoe fits,
wear it!"

I am indebted to a great many people for their co-
operation and time spent in interviews and discussions
concerning karate history. Individual acknowledgment

would be an impossibility. Special thanks, on the other hand, must be given to the following people for aid above and beyond that expected or even hoped for: to Dr. Minoru Shinoda for his patience in guiding me through the rigors of a graduate thesis; to the Reverend Dr. James Mitose for his several years of friendship and the telling of his personal experiences in pioneering his form of self-defense in Hawaii; to Dr. Benjamin Stone at the University of Malaya for his source materials on Malayan *bersilat;* to messrs. Rudy Ter Linden and Paul de Thouars, Indonesian fighting experts, who have graciously spent hours in demonstrating and speaking of their native combat arts; to Editor Chinei Kinjo, of the Okinawan *Yoen Jiho Sha* in Honolulu, for his time spent in gathering data on Okinawan karate pioneers in the Hawaiian Islands; to May Choye, Akio Inoue, and James Umeda, for their hours spent in helping me translate Chinese and Japanese sources; to my old instructors, Masaichi Oshiro, George Miyasaki, and Kenneth Murakami, for their help in giving me the basics of karate; to karate *sensei* Tsutomu Ohshima, for assisting me in finding the historical karate ties in California; and lastly, to my old friend Richard E. White, whose editorial advice and suggestions made this whole publication a reality.

B. A. HAINES

South Pasadena, California

Chapter 1

Introduction &
Terminology

In the sixth century, China was approaching her zenith as the most "cultured" and powerful nation on earth. China's suzerainty over her immediate neighbors was absolute. She exacted tribute not only from these bordering states, but also from countries hundreds of miles from her periphery, and was thus recognized as the central power of the globe.

As early as the Shang dynasty (*ca.* 1766–1122 B.C.), Arabian camel caravans roamed freely between west-central Asia and China proper, enabling the Middle East, and later the West, to enjoy Chinese products such as silk, tea, porcelain, paper, and gunpowder, the so-called "five great treasures of old Cathay." That these caravans were able to successfully traverse these difficult and often dangerous routes is a tribute to the Arabs' skill and their ability to defend themselves against constant bandit attacks. Their fighting ability was due in no small way to their exposure to both the great powers of the East and of the West, and to their eclectic abilities in borrowing the best of the combat techniques from each.

China did not solicit Western goods. But, as the major power of Asia, she felt obligated to return her satellites' tribute gifts with favors of greater measure and value.

Thus far more material wealth left China than was brought in; however, in this process of material exploitation, two unique gifts were to find their way into China which would greatly alter her cultural heritage.

Traveling out of India in approximately A.D. 525, an obscure Buddhist monk named Bodhidharma crossed the Chinese frontier[1]* and entered a land already exposed to Theravada and Mahayana doctrines, the two major schools of Buddhist philosophy. This self-appointed religious mission, of seemingly little consequence, is monumental when viewed in its historical perspective. In most of East Asia today, this Indian monk is revered as the spiritual father of Zen Buddhism and the founder of a weaponless fighting art which was the precursor of modern-day karate.

The term "karate" has been widely known in the Western world for little more than five years. To some, the word has almost a religious connotation; for others it evokes images of physical violence such as the bare-handed breaking of bricks and boards, and combat between man and man or man and beast. But regardless of the viewpoint, the important fact is that karate has become a very real part of Western life and holds the promise of becoming thoroughly integrated into Western culture. Unfortunately, most of those who have, until now, attempted to exploit this tremendous interest in karate have relied on unauthoritative sources for their information. This is sadly attested to by the many karate students and teachers who, with little or no first-hand knowledge of this art's beginnings and development, freely "explain" it to inter-

---

* These numbers refer to Notes & Sources to be found in the back of the book.

ested members of the press and television, and to magazine journalists.

Karate is basically an art or practice of self-defense in which only the bare hands, arms, and feet are used. In this respect it is similar to judo and *sumo* wrestling. Its chief point of departure from the others is that karate emphasizes the kick, the open-handed strike, and the closed fist strike rather than the take-down, the hold, and the throw. So effective is this form of self-defense that it is said a karate master can defend himself against a great number of adversaries, human or animal.

Karate has developed to a high degree of proficiency on Okinawa and Japan and multitudes of karate schools are found throughout these islands. On the Japanese university campus in particular, karate is becoming as traditional as the professorial lecture and the writing of term papers.

Terminology

It is commonly held that karate developed either in Japan proper, or on Okinawa during the time that it was a rather formidable island kingdom. But, careful scrutiny of Asian history reveals overwhelming proof that karate-like arts existed in various parts of Asia long before they were known in either Japan or Okinawa.

In the present-day Japanese language the ideographs for karate are 空手, meaning "empty hand" and are pronounced [kah-rah-tay] with equal emphasis on each syllable. Prior to the 20th century various terms were used in Chinese and Japanese to describe certain fighting techniques that existed on Okinawa and which had marked similarities to modern karate. The Japanese reading of some of these techniques are *kempo* 拳法, *tode* 唐手, and *te* 手.[2]

It happens that the term "kempo" means "law of the fist" or "way of the fist" and is read *ch'üan fa* in Mandarin and *ken fat* in Cantonese. It designates a Chinese form of self-defense and self-development very similar to karate. This in itself implies a probable connection between the two forms.

"Tode" is another term suggestive of Chinese influence on karate. The first character *to* 唐 of *tode* is the symbol for T'ang, the name of the great Chinese dynasty which flourished between A.D. 618–906 and which influenced Japan in many ways. In fact, so great was the admiration of the T'ang by Japan that in the centuries which followed the demise of this great dynasty, the character *to,* which is also read as *kara,* was used as an adjective meaning "China." The ideographic combination 唐手 can thus be read either as "tode" or "karate."

Te simply means "hand." However, as early as 1629 this term was used on Okinawa to describe a fighting style which bears a strong resemblance to modern karate.[3]

The use of the ideograph 空 to stand for *kara* is, as we shall see, a 20th-century development. In 1905 karate was included in the physical education curriculum of Okinawa's intermediate schools. The ideographs 唐手, pronounced [kah-rah-tay], were standard on Okinawa at this time.[4] In 1906 an Okinawan karate master named Chomo Hanagi broke from this traditional way of writing karate and used the other *kara* 空 ideograph for his book, *Karate Soshu Hen.*[5] This work is the first written record in which *kara* is represented by a different written character.

In October, 1936, the Okinawan newspaper *Ryukyu Shimpo Sha* sponsored a meeting of the great Okinawan karate masters Yabu, Kiyamu, Motobu, Miyagi, and Hanagi, in Naha, capital city of Okinawa.[6] The purpose of the meeting was to discuss certain aspects of karate, including the use of the T'ang character in writing karate, and its implications concerning the art.[7] It was decided that the *kara* 空 ideograph was best suited for the writing of the word, both because this ideograph was closely associated with Buddhist philosophy (see Chapter Seven) and because in dispensing with the *to* 唐 ideograph they would erase the Chinese association. The result of this meeting was that by 1937 the 空手 form of writing karate became standardized and has remained unchanged to the present day.[8]

Besides the Okinawan and Chinese prototypes described above, there were five fighting techniques that may have contributed to modern-day karate. They were: Egyptian bare-handed fighting as depicted in pyramid wall murals; Roman gladiatorial combat; Japanese *sumo* wrestling; Indian and Persian foot fighting; and a genus of weaponless fighting found in Thailand, Malaysia, Cambodia, Laos, and Vietnam.[9] Even though there is no apparent link between the five techniques, karate contains elements of all of them. The implication, of course, is that karate must have developed in a country that carried on an active and extensive intercourse with the West as well as with all of Asia. The finger of logic points inevitably to China, although India appears to have been the birthplace for some archaic forms of weaponless combat.

Chapter 2

India

INDIA had traditionally veiled herself in a cloak of pacifism until shortly after Word War II. Mahatma Ghandi's non-violent struggle for independence from England in the 1930's and 1940's led to the popular belief that India was intrinsically and historically anti-military. This is not an accurate assumption. Warfare was, in fact, an integral part of early Indian culture.

Numerous kingdoms of various sizes dotted the sub-continent in pre-Christian times, each vying with one another for local supremacy. Warfare was thrust upon the people and all types of combat formed a special niche in India's earlier civilizations. A warrior class called the *Kshátriya,* who can best be compared to the Japanese *samurai* and the medieval knights of Europe, were the then dominant strata in Indian society.

This military group antedates Buddhism and played the leading role in the development of Indian culture until the rise of the Brahmin or priest caste. Despite the difficulty in accurately pinpointing the evolvement of a karate-like art at this early date, we shall see that the *Kshátriya* had a direct relationship with at least one early fighting style.

The first written evidence of an Indian bare-handed

fighting art is mentioned in the well-known Buddhist scripture called the *Lotus Sutra*.* In Chapter 14 an interesting passage is cited where the historic Buddha, speaking to a follower called Manjusri, says, "In the sphere of action and intimacy the bodhisattva dwells in a state of patience . . . he seeks no intimacy with kings, princes . . . nor with heretics . . . nor with pugilists. . . ."[1] As pugilism is the art or practice of fighting with fists, the Buddha's comment seems clearly to indicate that a karate-like art existed before or during the writing of the *Lotus Sutra*.

The Chinese translation of the *Lotus Sutra*, read *Fa Hua San Ch'ing*, is the most widely accredited version in present-day Asia. Here, the aforementioned pugilistic art is called *hsiang ch'a hsiang p'u* 相乂相撲.[2] The two ideographs 相乂 mean "mutual striking" or "mutual pounding." The other part of the ideographic combination 相撲 means so nearly the same thing that the best translation of the whole phrase is simply "mutual striking." This confirms the Sanskrit translation's indication of a weaponless martial art or sporting combat.

The characters 相撲 are also used in Japanese. But there they represent the ancient art of *sumo* wrestling, a subject to be discussed later (see Chapter Six).

Returning to the *Lotus Sutra*, we find reference to another fighting art called *nata* 那羅.[3] According to one standard Sanskrit-English dictionary the word *nata* means "a manly character; a dancer or performer."[4] Its use is significant because there is a close similarity between

---

* The *Lotus Sutra*, author unknown, is called the *Hokke-kyo* in Japanese and *Saddharma Pundarika* in Sanskrit. It is assumed to have been written in Sanskrit somewhere in northern India. The best English translation is William Soothill's *The Lotus of the Wonderful Law*.

Oriental dancing and the martial arts of *ch'üan fa* and karate. *Ch'üan fa,* as was noted previously, is a Chinese style of weaponless fighting closely related to karate. Both of these forms have sets of prescribed exercise and practice movements very similar to shadow boxing in modern pugilism. An untrained observer watching an art similar to *ch'üan fa* for the first time might well believe the practitioner to be dancing. *Nata,* therefore, may not be dancing, but in actuality a fighting technique akin to karate or *ch'üan fa.*[5]

Continuing with the proof that a bare-handed fighting art existed in ancient India, we find further reference in an early Buddhist sutra called the *Hongyo-kyo.*[6] Herein is described a "strength contest" between a Prince Nanda and a Devadatta. Prince Nanda was the half brother of Gautama, the historic Buddha, while Devadatta is thought of as the jealous cousin of the Buddha.[7]

Although we cannot determine with certainty whether this story is fact or myth, the important point for our purpose is that this citation refers to these tests of combat, mentioned frequently in early Indian works. This supports the fact that more than one type of weaponless fighting was extant and was being popularly practiced in India before cropping up in either Chinese or Japanese literature.

India appears to be the birthplace of yet another early bare-handed martial art, *vájramushti.* Evidence seems to indicate that this was the very first karate-like technique and that it was commonly practiced by the previously mentioned *Kshátriya,* or warrior caste. *Vájramushti* is translated as "one whose clenched fist is . . . adamant; of a *Kshátriya,* or warrior; the clenched fist as a weapon."[8]

One modern karate authority, in describing *vájramushti*

practice, states that students of this art strengthened their hands by first pouring milk on their fists or by immersing the whole hand into milk, and then striking a slab of marble repeatedly with the knuckles.[9] In India, milk has significance as an object of religious veneration and it is uncertain whether the practice of dipping the fist into milk before striking a punching stone was for religious or medicinal purposes or both.

Most contemporary schools of karate likewise emphasize training of the knuckles by fist striking, some going so far as to use specially prepared Chinese medicines to heal the knuckle skin which inevitably bruises and splits open as a result of overzealous training on the punching board

It is certain that there was some type of weaponless fighting practiced in early Buddhistic India, judging the data that is now available. Mendicant Buddhist monks are said to have utilized both the arts of *hsiang ch'a hsiang p'u* and *vájramushti*.[10] Though the evidence for such an assumption is not abundant, it is interesting to note such an association of a violent martial art with the usually tranquil spirit of Buddhism. This association becomes exceedingly complex as the history of karate unfolds.

One last theory that tends to identify karate with Indian bare-handed fighting is based on the Buddhist statuary of India. Many of the postures of early Indian works have a marked resemblance to karate forms.[11] This applies particularly to the eleven-headed, thousand-armed *Kwannon* which is a Buddhist mythical deity found in many Japanese temples. Lastly, the statues of the so-called *Nio* deities, also found in Buddhist temples of Japan, display unmistakable similarities to karate.

These *Nio Bodhisattvas,* replicas of earlier Indian pro-

1. A Japanese *Nio* guardian deity glares fiercely and threatens with the karate *seiken* (closed) fist. This type of Buddhist art dates back into Indian antiquity and gives relevance to the claim that karate originated in India. *Photograph by Yoshio Shimada.*

totypes, are the protectors of the Buddhist faith and are often called by the Sanskrit term of *Vira* (or *Vájraprani*) and the Japanese word *Kongorishiki.*[12] A large number of these statues are found as guardians in the gate entrances to Buddhist temples, usually in an exact karate stance.

Although none of the foregoing bits of evidence can be considered conclusive proof that a form of karate existed in ancient India, taken as a whole they point so overwhelmingly to such a conclusion that it is impossible to think otherwise. As we shall now see, this germinal idea was taken into China and nurtured into an empty-handed fighting art so formidable that its exponents were referred to with a reverential air.

Chapter 3

China

CHINA, like India, has been the nurturing spot for numerous martial art forms. While some of these arts were actually initiated in China, many were brought in from other countries and so Sinicized after centuries of practice in China that today they appear to be of Chinese inspiration.

It is difficult, even with access to reams of statistical data, to determine bases or patterns for behavior, and the task is enormously amplified when the behavioral patterns were established hundreds of years in the past. For this reason, it cannot be authoritatively determined why the earliest *ch'üan fa* schools were so secretive that it was considered a capital offense to display the techniques to the uninitiated. This particular behavior pattern has made extremely difficult the task of the historian studying Chinese weaponless martial arts.

In the field of weaponless combat, China undoubtedly was the catalyst in producing the techniques that have eventually come to be called karate. While the major Chinese precursor of karate is *ch'üan fa* in Mandarin Chinese, it is more popularly known as *kung-fu* [pronounced "gung-foo"]. Although we call *ch'üan fa* a Chinese art, it is doubtful that it is wholly a product of Chinese genius.

23

We know, for example, that from India's influence on China there arose at least one form of bare-handed fighting, the pioneer of which was the Indian monk, Bodhidharma.

Bodhidharma is an obscure figure in history. The most reliable sources for our knowledge of the man are generally considered to be *Biographies of the High Priests* by Priest Tao-hsuan, written in A.D. 654, and the *Records of the Transmission of the Lamp,* by Priest Tao-yuan, written in 1004.[1] But the earliest written source concerning Bodhidharma is found in a work entitled *Records of the Lo-yang Temple,* by Yang Hsuan-chih in 547.[2] These seemingly authentic sources notwithstanding, however, modern scholarship has been either reluctant to accept any single version of Bodhidharma's existence, or it asserts that all accounts of the Indian monk are legendary (see Paul Pelliot in *T'oung Pao,* 1923). On the other hand, eminent Buddhist-historians such as D. T. Suzuki, Kenneth Ch'en, and Heinrich Dumoulin, feel that Bodhidharma was an actual person despite the many admitted sprinklings and spicings of myth that have been added to his biography.

Bodhidharma was the third child of King Sugandha in southern India,[3] was a member of the *Kshátriya,* or warrior caste,[4] and had his childhood in Conjeeveram[5] (also, Kanchipuram, Kancheepuram), the small but dynamically Buddhist province south of Madras. He is said to have received his religious training from the *dhyana* master, Prajnatara, who was responsible for changing the young disciple's name from Bodhitara.[6] An apt pupil, Bodhidharma soon exceeded his contemporaries so that by the time of his middle age, he was considered to be very wise in the ways of *dhyana,* or Zen practices. When Prajnatara died, Bodhidharma set sail for China, possibly because of a death-bed wish from his old master, according to the *Records of Lo-yang Temple*.[7] On the other hand, Tao-yuan's *Records of the Transmission of the Lamp* indicate that the decision to go to China was made by Bodhidharma alone, because he was saddened by the decline of Buddhism in the areas outside of India proper.[8]

Accounts of Bodhidharma's activities in China vary considerably with the reference cited. Tao-hsuan's *Biographies of the High Priests* states that Bodhidharma first arrived in China during the Sung dynasty (420–479) of the Southern Dynasties (420–589), and later traveled north to the Kingdom of Wei.[9] But the traditional date of Bodhidharma's entry into China has been 520 (*vars.*, 526, 527). This appears to be rather late if Tao-hsuan's *Biographies* . . . is accurate in placing him at the Yung-ning Temple at Lo-Yang in 520.[10] *Biographies* . . . further states that a Buddhist "novice" called Seng-fu joined Bodhidharma's following, was ordained by Bodhidharma after an undisclosed period of study, and then left to journey to south China where he passed away in 524 at the age of sixty-one.[11] Basic mathematics tells us that if Seng-fu were, indeed, sixty-one in 524, and had been the minimum acceptable age for ordination (20 years old at that time) when so honored by Bodhidharma, he would have been twenty in *ca.* 483, putting the Indian monk in China considerably earlier than the traditional date of 520.[12]

A variation of the above theory, found in the *Records of the Transmission of the Lamp* (1004), places Bodhidharma in Canton in 527. After some time there, he traveled northward, meeting the Emperor Wu of the Liang dynasty (502–557) at Chin-ling (now Nanking).[13] It was at this time that the now-famous question-and-answer dialogue took place between the learned monk and Emperor Wu. Realizing that his form of *dhyana* "questioning" was of little avail with the pious but worldly monarch, Bodhidharma left the court for the Shaolin Monastery,[14] where significant events then took place.

Bodhidharma's meeting with Liang Wu-ti appears neither in the *Records of the Lo-yang Temple* nor in the *Biographies . . . ,*[15] written in 547 and 654 respectively. Since the *Records of the Transmission of the Lamp* was compiled 350 years after the *Biographies . . . ,* when Zen practices had already been well established in China, it is possible that the Bodhidharma-Emperor Wu debate was invented as a reverent allegory for explaining specific Zen tenets. Again there are insufficient historical correlations to enable us to draw a firmly based conclusion.

After the famous but historically questionable encounter between Bodhidharma and Emperor Wu, Bodhidharma's life is centered around the Shaolin Temple and Monastery located in Honan Province. Tradition states that upon seeing the emaciated condition of the monks of this temple, Bodhidharma instructed them in physical exercises to condition their bodies as well as their minds.[16]

In several works dealing with *ch'üan fa* and its Okinawan counterpart, karate, reference is made to the close tie between Bodhidharma's Shaolin exercises and the above-named fighting arts. The factual basis for these hypotheses is the series of physical drills Bodhidharma introduced to the Shaolin monks, called *shih pa lo han sho,*[17] or in English, "Eighteen Hands of the Lo-Han."

At the present time *Lo-Han* is used to designate all famous disciples of the historic Buddha, but more generally the term refers to those five hundred *arhats* (Sanskrit term for those who have achieved Nirvana) who are supposed to reappear on earth as Buddhas,[18] according to Buddhist mythology in some sects of the religion.

The precise meaning of Lo-Han in Bodhidharma's time, however, is lost, and we are forced to rely on the educated assumption that they were some form of temple guardians of Hindu origin.[19] It also appears that their original Hindu number was sixteen, and that the Chinese added two to bring the total to eighteen.[20]

According to E. T. C. Werner in his monumental *Dictionary of Chinese Mythology,* there does not appear to be any historical account of the first introduction of the *Lo-Han* into the halls of Buddhist temples. Werner goes on to state that the eighteen *Lo-Han* did not exist before the time of a Buddhist poet and artist named Kuan-hsiu (832–912). However, we have already seen that martial arts tradition states that the *shih pa lo han sho* were introduced at the Shaolin Monastery sometime after 520, thus designating Bodhidharma as the initiator of the term "Lo-Han" in the Chinese culture.

For our purposes, however, the main significance of the *shih pa lo han sho,* via Bodhidharma, is that it is reputed to be the basis for the famous Shaolin *ch'üan fa.*[21]

This theory, on the other hand, raises a number of questions. For example, Bodhidharma's chief concern was apparently to cultivate the minds of his followers so that enlightenment could be achieved. Why would a Zen patriarch conceive a form of *ch'üan fa,* which, at least in its present stage of evolution, is a brutally effective weapon of combat? The answer, most probably, is that Bodhidharma never intended his *shih pa lo han sho* to be a violent martial art. There is certainly nothing to be found in the Bodhidharma image, as portrayed in the existing references, that would connect him with the later slapping, striking, punching, grunting, and generally violent masters of Zen Buddhism.

Here is an interesting hypothesis that has been overlooked by historians to date. The term traditionally applied to Bodhidharma—"wall gazing Brahmin"—is a misnomer. Reliable accounts (e.g., Chou's *A History of Chinese Buddhism,* Werner's *Dictionary of Chinese Mythology,* etc.) show that Bodhidharma was a member of the *Kshátriya* or warrior caste in India. As such, he was exposed to all existing forms of weaponless fighting from boyhood. The *Kshátriya*'s most notable bare-handed fighting technique was called *vájramushti,* which is translated as: "one whose clenched fist is . . . adamant; of a *Kshátriya,* or warrior; the clenched fist as a weapon."[22] Mendicant Buddhist monks as well as the *Kshátriya* are said to have utilized *vájramushti* techniques,[23] and there is little doubt that as a *Kshátriya* in India and later a peripatetic monk in China, Bodhidharma learned this technique of fighting. Whether the *shih pa lo han sho* is specifically an extension of *vájramushti* forms will probably never be known, since little has been written about the development of *vájramushti* per se, and references linking Bodhidharma with "self-defense" techniques are scarce. Tao-hsuan's *Biographies of the High Priests* (654) fails to mention Bodhidharma in connection with anything that could be linked to martial arts. Of course, this omission does not mean that Bodhidharma did not introduce the Shaolin monks to some unique physical and perhaps martial art, especially since few academicians have taken an active interest in the mundane martial arts associated with historical events, and several of the most careful historians who hold strong reputations for accuracy in defining "things Oriental" have "missed the boat," so to speak, when classifying all Asian combat forms as simply "boxing" or "pugilism."

The development of the Shaolin style of unarmed self-defense, though popularly associated with Bodhidharma, has a varied history, again depending on the source. The most plausible version indicates that after Bodhidharma left the monastery, many of the other monks of the Shaolin set out to disseminate his teachings. Contrary to the belief of D. T. Suzuki and others, the martial arts tradition which surrounds Bodhidharma attributed two books to his genius which were found a short while after his demise, secreted in the walls of the temple.[24]

The first work, entitled *Hsi Sui Chin* was said to have been transcribed by Bodhidharma's disciple Hui K'o[25] and has since been lost to the world. The second work, *I-Chin-ching,* has been translated several times and clouding this work is the possibility that it is a forgery from a period well after Bodhidharma's death. Tradition has it that these writings are not only filled with the spirit of Zen Buddhism, but that they also reveal Bodhidharma's position on physical activity as a means of body hygienics. The dubious nature of these writings, however, makes them unacceptable as conclusive historical documents.

Several decades after the death of Bodhidharma a certain *ch'üan fa* master named Ch'ueh Yuan shang-jen verified the existence of Bodhidharma's "Eighteen Hands of the Lo Han" exercise and combined these movements with numerous forms of his own style.[26] The obscurity surrounding the life of Ch'ueh Yuan shang-jen is no less than that which is present in nearly every work dealing with *ch'üan fa.* The existing biographical data on him tells us little more than that he came from either Honan or

Shantung Province. But our interest in him is not in his biography but in the fact that he is credited with increasing Bodhidharma's original eighteen hand-and-foot positions to seventy-two.[27]

After Ch'ueh had spent some time popularizing his expanded version of the Shaolin *ch'üan fa,* he traveled to Shensi Province where he met with another martial arts master named Li. Ch'ueh and Li are said to have enlarged the seventy-two strokes to one-hundred and seventy, and to have given the best of these movements such names as dragon, tiger, snake, and crane.

The authoritarian French source *La Médecine Chinoise Au Cours Des Siécles* refers to the previously mentioned Ch'ueh Yuan shang-jen as Kiao Yuan, claiming that it was he who initiated the additional movements to the *shih pa lo han sho* (up to 173 movements) and gave to it a decalog of moral precepts. Whether Ch'ueh Yuan and Kiao Yuan are one and the same is not known, as the Romanization of the two surnames gives nearly the same pronunciation. At any rate, it was Ch'ueh Yuan (or Kiao Yuan) who was responsible for the rise and fame of the Shaolin *ch'üan fa,*[28] and therein is where our interest lies.

Most *ch'üan fa* forms practiced in the 20th century are descendents of the one-hundred seventy (*var.* 173) hand-and-foot positions of Ch'ueh Yuan, and though they have undergone a steady evolution they can still be traced ultimately to Bodhidharma's embryonic eighteen positions. Yet one more historical episode exists that clouds even this well-authenticated conclusion. During the Sui period (589–618), brigands attacked the Shaolin Monastery.[29] Various futile attempts were made by the resident monks to protect themselves until at last one priest called the "begging monk" drove off the outlaws with a virtuosity of kicking and punching styles. This performance so impressed the other monks that they asked the "begging monk" to instruct them in his fighting form, which later developed into the famous Shaolin *ch'üan fa*.

Since the popular version in Japan and most of Asia persists that it was Bodhidharma who founded the Shaolin *ch'üan fa*, some readers may mistakenly associate the "begging monk" with Bodhidharma. This assumption is immediately ruled out, however, when we see that the "begging monk" lived during the Sui period which began in A.D. 589, and well after Bodhidharma's death (*ca.* 534). Hence, the account of the so-called "begging monk" seems to represent a conflicting version of the founding of the Shaolin *ch'üan fa*.

Regardless of one's motives in favoring one account over the other, there are too many references in favor of the Bodhidharma legend to make other narratives truly convincing. In all probability, this spiritual pioneer of Zen in China can be credited with the founding of at least one form of the Shaolin style of *ch'üan fa*. But, as the major task of revising Bodhidharma's original eighteen-stroke exercise to one-hundred seventy offensive and defensive movements belongs to the previously cited *ch'üan fa* master, Ch'ueh Yuan shang-jen, we deduce that *ch'üan fa*, as a truly lethal military art, developed with this man.

The Shaolin *ch'üan fa* is the first school of bare-handed fighting listed under the general heading of "External School" or *Wai Chia* 外家.[30] The "External School" is the major classification under which eight other styles are grouped.[31] The exact date of origin for this terminology is not known. It was probably used at first to categorize various types of *ch'üan fa* under one heading after the Shaolin style came into existence.

The other eight forms listed under the "External School" are: *Hung Ch'üan* and *T'au T'ei Yu T'an T'ui* both from the Sung period (A.D. 1127–1279); the *Hon Ch'üan, Erh-lang Men, Fan Ch'üan,* and *Ch'a Ch'üan* styles dated from the Ming dynasty (A.D. 1368–1644)—the latter form used exclusively by Chinese Moslems; and two styles attributed to the Ch'ing period (A.D. 1644–1911), called *Mi Tsung Yi* and *Pa Ch'üan.*[32]

In nearly every instance, the founders of these eight *ch'üan fa* styles were said to have been Taoist deities or demi-gods. The real creators of these various forms appear to be lost to the world and, as the so-called godlike inventors are timeless entities in the mythology of China, many Chinese believe that *ch'üan fa* has always existed. Historically dating the first public display of the above named styles of *ch'üan fa* has thus far been impossible. The importance of the *ch'üan fa*-Taoist association will be discussed later (Chapter Seven).

The same obscurity found in the history of the "External School" is likewise seen in the background of the "Internal School" of *ch'üan fa,* called *Nei Chia* 内家. These forms are all from Sung or post-Sung dynasty dates and are called: *Wu Tang P'ai, T'ai Ch'i Ch'üan, Pa Kua Ch'üan, Hsin Yi Ch'üan, Tzu Jan Men,* and *Liu He Pa Fa.*[33]

Bodhidharma's final days are shrouded in the mystery of marvelous and supernatural events. After transmitting the "dharma" to his disciple Hui K'o at the Shaolin Temple, one version has it that he died and was neatly and properly buried on Hsiung-erh Shan (Bear's Ear Hill),[34] in Honan Province. Those who ascribe to this "neat and proper" theory vary in his death date between 529 and 535.[35] However, we then encounter a work entitled *Shen-hsien t'ung-chien,*[36] wherein a Wei official en route to Central Asia for a good-will mission reported a cordial meeting with Bodhidharma at Ch'ung-lin (Onion Range) in the Belaturgh Mountains of Turkestan. Carrying a single sandal, Bodhidharma was asked by the official where he was going, to which the monk replied: "I am going back to the Western Heaven [India]."[37]

This tale was later reported to the Wei Emperor who accordingly exhumed Bodhidharma's tomb, wherein he found . . . one sandal.[38] The emperor, awed by this "resurrection," attempted to preserve the surviving foot garment in the Shaolin Monastery, but even it disappeared (reportedly stolen) before the passage of two centuries.[39]

Bodhidharma's final exit in Chinese history under such strange circumstances is certainly in character with the general mode of sixth-century Chinese thought. Mysticism, magic, and supernatural entities were the "stuff" of which early Chinese folklore, and postfirst-century Buddhist religious thought, were made.

There is every possibility that some type of weaponless combat developed in China long before the advent of Bodhidharma. According to one authority, a certain form of *ch'üan fa* evolved in China approximately five thousand years ago during the reign of the semi-mythical Yellow Emperor, Huang-ti.[40]

2.   Earthenware figurine of the Han dynasty (209 B.C.-A.D. 24) in a stance identical to a *ch'üan fa* position.

There is further reference to the birth of this art in the dynastic history known as the *Han Shu* (Han dynasty 209 B.C.–A.D. 24), but the date ascribed to it is much too remote in antiquity to be convincing. Thus, other than saying that something akin to *ch'üan fa*-karate developed very early in China, we can make no definitive statements about its beginning.

Secret societies have played an important role in Chinese history from earliest times; however, the first outspokenly anti-government group existed near the end of the Han dynasty, called the "Carnation Eyebrow Rebels."[41] Because of the effectiveness of this society in accomplishing its aims, the list of such organizations grew until eventually wherever political oppression became intolerable, or a foreign power came to rule (such as the Mongols of Marco Polo's time), these secret societies led the fight in restoring desirable government.

Since 1644 a foreign Manchu dynasty had controlled China's destiny, subjecting the multitudes of Chinese to the role of second-class citizens. Agitation for reform and overthrow of the Manchu autocracy brought swift reprisals to participants therein. So, to end this government oppression, Chinese secret societies went "underground" and became the leading protagonists for anti-Manchu activity.

The Ch'ing dynasty (1644–1911) of the Manchus thus became a leading target for revolutionary activities of various groups, with the famous and powerful "White Lotus Society" heading the attempted coup, which included such secret anti-Manchu groups as the "Three Incense Sticks," "The Rationalist Society," and the "Eight Diagrams."[42]

Then, in the middle of the 19th century, Western powers began their long-anticipated economic and military assault on the "Middle Kingdom." A beleaguered China, proud of her ancient civilization and scornful of the Occidental "barbarians," was unsuccessful in forestalling European aggression and final victory. England led the way in opening China's sealed doors, forcing her to war in 1839 and 1856, with the French joining the British in the latter encounter. These involvements cost China the island of Hong Kong which was ceded to the British for war reparations, as well as numerous "treaty ports" on the Chinese mainland, not to mention various other "rights" and advantages.

Western imperialism was at first only a minor irritation to the general mass of Chinese people for whom foreign invasion was an expected part of life. In the past millennia of Chinese history the transgressors had eventually left China of their own accord or, being Mongoloid peoples, they were assimilated into the Chinese culture and not thought of as invaders. The foreign Manchus, though in control of China for nearly three hundred years, had been oppressive rulers and Chinese hatred was centered on the Manchu dynasty. However, after the Opium War of 1839, England and all other foreign "barbarians" slowly became the objects of Chinese animosity. After a time the United States joined additional European nations in obtaining similar guarantees in China.[43] By the beginning of the 20th century Chinese sovereignty had virtually ceased to exist.

Hatred of Western domination reached a breaking point in 1900 when the Boxers staged their famous rebellion. The significance of this revolt for our purposes lies in the fact that the Boxers represent a type of *ch'üan fa* activity.

The term "Boxers" was first applied to *ch'üan fa* cultists

by Westerners in China when they saw a similarity between *ch'üan fa* and their own brands of pugilistic encounter. And, although very few *ch'üan fa* schools seem to have participated in the Boxer Rebellion, they became lumped together under the term "Boxers" which eventually was used by the invading Westerners to indicate any Chinese secret society or group that demonstrated hatred of the West. One large group of Boxers, and it seems that this society was more responsible for the term "Boxers" than any other, was called the *I-Ho-Ch'üan* or "Righteous and Harmonious Fists," of which only a small portion were *ch'üan fa* practitioners. The *I-Ho-Ch'üan* was a branch of an older secret organization, the aforementioned "Eight Diagrams," founded near the close of the Ming dynasty. This "Eight Diagrams" was probably not a *ch'üan fa* association either, but affiliated with it were certain *ch'üan fa* groups such as the *I-Ho-Ch'üan*. The "Eight Diagrams" society became a leading anti-Western clique before and during the short Boxer war of 1900.[44]

Two other Boxer groups which may have had strong *ch'üan fa* membership were the *K'an* and *Ch'ien* Boxers.[45] These two groups were active in northern China during the 1900 rebellion and were associated with both the *I-Ho-Ch'üan* and the "Eight Diagrams."[46] Besides the more clandestine activities of the various secret societies, the 1900 war also attracted multitudes of Chinese men, both young and old, who formed into bands of "gymnasts"[47] and who practiced numerous forms of *ch'üan fa*.

In retrospect, the Boxer Rebellion was an unorganized mass revolt against foreign controls in China. The amount of actual *ch'üan fa* activity was slight, although the ruling Manchu aristocracy and the peasantry seemed to have been mesmerized by *ch'üan fa* performers into believing that they could outdo the mighty Western military science with their weaponless art. It is interesting to note that the appeal of *ch'üan fa* was sufficient to enlist the masses in this revolt against the foreign elements, in spite of the knowledge that their opponents would be retaliating with every type of firearm in their possession. As it turned out, most of the actual combat during the rebellion was conducted with weapons. The empty-handed or true *ch'üan fa* styles seem to have been employed primarily for propaganda purposes.

> For two months, from June 20 to August 14, (1900), the Kansu Army of Tung Fu-hsing and hundreds of 'righteous' people flourished all sorts of magic weapons such as soul-absorbing banners, sky-covering flags, thunderbolt fans, and flying swords. They succeeded in killing only one important person, the German Minister Von Ketteler.[48]

*　　　*　　　*　　　*

In every true art form, whether aesthetic or practical, some part of the artist's technique is kept secret. This is especially true of Chinese *ch'üan fa*. Even at the present time, ancient *ch'üan fa* is kept in relative secrecy among the physical culture clubs that practice this art. In the past five years in the United States, *ch'üan fa* secrecy and selectivity have appeared to diminish somewhat, so that whereas before only those of pure Chinese ancestry were accepted as students, now all racial groups can be found studying the art. However, upon closer scrutiny it can be seen that many techniques normally included in *ch'üan fa* are excluded from the open teachings, and are

3.   *Ch'üan fa* brought up to date! Ages-old movements in traditional and modern garb.

taught to those of Chinese ancestry at a different time or in a separate location.

The 20th century, far from witnessing the demise of *ch'üan fa* has seen a great rise in its popularity. In Communist China, Mao Tse-tung has utilized the appeal of *ch'üan fa* to enlist participants in his gymnastic program, as well as for a pragmatic form of self-defense that everyone is urged to learn. Numerous Chinese "boxing" magazines are printed in Red China and Hong Kong, with thousands of readers found throughout the Chinese communities of the world.

4. Figures from the famous Mai-Chi-Shan caves in China showing statuary in *ch'üan fa* positions, particularly the figure on the right. There is reason to believe that carvings of this nature are representative of the type now called *lo-han* in China.

From the foregoing it can be seen why the recent opening of *ch'üan fa* doors to Westerners has met with such opposition from certain *ch'üan fa* societies. Of course, those who have taken the step usually claim that they teach non-Chinese participants only a watered-down version of the true art, and that the "secrets" have never been divulged to the Western world. So, though it appears that *kung-fu* (the common term for *ch'üan fa* in the West) is becoming a universal art along with the other karate-like styles of self-defense, it is possible that we will never see it practiced as it once was in the fabled temples of Shaolin.

Chapter 4

Southeast Asia

MARTIAL art development is largely based on imitation followed by periods and degrees of refinement. That is, most newly forming societies look to countries with an already-established system of fighting for guides in developing their own military organizations. Few peoples have been inventive enough to develop original concepts of combat, especially in the realm of empty-handed fighting. Thus, as weaponless martial arts systems have long existed in Southeast Asia, the problem of where, when, and how they evolved becomes very important to the martial arts historian.

Southeast Asia is at the same time a land of fabled romance, myth, and legend, and one of monotonous sameness. Much blessed in natural resources, it is a land where the people of many diverse cultures generally have lived easily from the earth's abundance, seldom experiencing the tragedy of starvation of their nearby East Asian neighbors. The patterns of life are generally unhurried and simple, and have been little affected by the vagaries of world political struggles until very recently, though the arm of colonial tyranny did reach out to choke off the initiative of the native peoples in many areas of Southeast Asia as early as the 16th century.

41

Such comparative self-sufficiency, coupled with the tropical languor so often found among peoples living in the earth's torrid regions, should probably have sufficed to prevent the development of serious fighting arts, since they demand such extremes of effort and self-discipline. However, as Southeast Asia had in ages past been the site of several magnificent civilizations, it did spawn numerous aesthetic and practical arts that are in every way equal to those developed by her East Asian neighbors—China, Korea, and Japan.

Only recently have students of Asian history "discovered" that empty-handed self-defense techniques have existed in Southeast Asia for hundreds of years. This is because they have been able to find so little written on the subject, and have thus had to rely on interviews with natives who are usually quite reluctant to speak about their arts. In fact, until archaeological expeditions hacked their way through the forbidding jungles and discovered structure after magnificent structure of former highly developed civilizations, there was no evidence whatsoever that verified the fact that such arts had been a part of Southeast Asian history. But slowly, after sifting carefully through the potpourri of wall carvings, temple friezes, and religious and secular statuary that so richly adorn these newly uncovered remains, the story of empty-handed martial art development has presented itself to those willing to investigate the record in stone.

Logically, we should approach the problem from two standpoints: First, from a consideration of the forms that are thought to be indigenous to Southeast Asia; and second, through an investigation of the styles which appear to be imported from outside of this geographic area.

Cambodia

Present-day Cambodia stands at the site where once flourished the famed Khmer Empire. For over six hundred years (A.D. 802–1432) the Khmers dominated much of Southeast Asia.[1] This great empire is said to have been the end result of a centuries-long migration of adventure-seeking "pioneers" from far-away India,[2] where imaginations had been inflamed by traders' stories of the immense wealth and unbelievable beauty of the "Land far to the East." As their isolation from "Mother India" grew more pronounced through the years, these people evolved a unique culture of their own. But because of the never-ceasing influx of Indian scholars and priests, the Khmer and the Indian were never entirely divorced.

A series of strong Khmer rulers restlessly expanded their territory, gathering the land's abundant fruits into an ever-burgeoning stockpile of riches, until soon the Khmer was recognized as one of the great cultural centers of Southeast Asia. Probably the most magnificent structures erected during this period were Suryavarman II's awe-inspiring temple of Angkor Wat, Jayavarman VII's walled city of Angkor Thom, and the strikingly detailed Bayon Temple.[3] It is in, on, and around the ruins of these now-decaying structures that a series of statues and animated reliefs are found depicting various phases of weaponless fighting.[4] In fact, figures portrayed in some form of close combat number in the thousands,[5] among which are many in fighting stances that are unmistakably of Chinese *ch'üan fa*.

The story that these statues tell is one of pronounced

5.   Clay statue in a *ch'üan fa* pose, found in the Terrace of the Elephants, Angkor Wat.

Chinese influence in early Southeast Asian history. This fact is well substantiated when we realize that it is from Chinese writings that most of our knowledge of the early Khmer comes, and that many of these writings are dated at the beginning of the Christian era.[6] A fascinating tale of peaceful exchange and interplay between two great kingdoms has unfolded from fragments pieced together only recently. Although we will not delve into it too deeply, suffice it to say that the earliest Khmer Kingdom, called Funan (A.D. 1 to 800), was visited regularly by Chinese traders and diplomatic envoys. That a very pronounced cultural exchange took place is attested to by Funan's sending a troop of Khmer musicians and dancers to entertain the Emperor of China in the third century.[7] These and other written facts offer the strong suggestion that many elements of early Khmer weaponless fighting were inspired by Chinese forms.

The early Indian arts of *hsiang ch'a hsiang p'u, nata,* and *vájramushti* seem to have no visual representation in Southeast Asia. By that we mean that no archaeological findings have yet indicated that these ancient Indian forms were introduced into Cambodia or elsewhere on the continental portion of Asia known geographically as "Southeast Asia." Thus although we know that there was a certain amount of intercourse between early India and Southeast Asia, we have no tangible evidence that early Khmer styles of fighting were descendents of any or all of the three above-cited Indian forms. And yet, since Indian ideas and practices flowed almost continuously into the Khmer Kingdom during the first millennium of the Khmer civilization,[8] it seems probable that India had a pronounced influence on the development of Khmer unarmed fighting. However, any conclusion based on the scanty evidence available would be historically hazardous.

The notion that many of the carvings and statues found in some form of unarmed fighting portray an original Khmer concept of bare-handed combat seems to be a logical deduction from the following facts: man has always used fists for weapons. The use of "hands" for fighting is seen even in highly evolved animals such as the kangaroo, bear, the big cats, and all of the primates. Boxing as a refined skill had its beginnings over twenty-five hundred years ago, as attested to by its inclusion in the Twenty-Third Olympiad in Greece (688 B.C.).[9] It became such a popular sport that it rather quickly reached a high level of development. Because of the naturalness with which such combat comes to man, it is reasonable to assume that the Khmers did devise their own form of bare-handed fighting. Thus the best assumption is that Khmer bare-handed fighting borrowed from both China and India, and gave to each in turn, but remained throughout a unique style unto itself.

Vietnam

This small, narrow country has the distinction of being the only Southeast Asian country under nearly constant Chinese subjugation for the past two thousand years.[10] The founding of the kingdom called "Nam-Viet" occurred in 208 B.C. and was composed of parts of present-day China and portions of what is now North Vietnam.[11] This kingdom, though independent in name, gave allegiance to the Han emperors of China.[12] Then, during one of China's expansion programs in 111 B.C., it was annexed and became an official part of China's "Middle Kingdom."

A form of *ch'üan fa* is practiced in modern Vietnam, but the exact time of its origin is not known. There is little doubt that this Vietnamese form was strongly influenced by the Chinese whose reign was so long and so all-encompassing.

Judo is also popularly pursued in present-day South Vietnam. The largest judo gymnasium in Saigon is, during most of each day, a wild scene of white-garbed judoists grappling and straining for victory under the watchful eyes of the founder of judo, Jigoro Kano, whose portrait is prominently displayed on the wall. Though judo came to Vietnam through Japanese influence, the Vietnamese call it by their own term, "nhu dao," which, like "judo," translates as "gentle way."[13]

A certain amount of Japanese influence in other areas of unarmed fighting undoubtedly took place during the Japanese occupation of the Indochina area during World War II, in spite of the fact that Japanese interest in

Southeast Asia was based entirely on economic considerations. For, although there is seldom a great deal of cultural exchange between victor and vanquished, there will always be found certain men who vigorously pursue new and untried physical activities that they feel will contribute to their self-improvement.

Little else can be said about weaponless martial arts in Vietnam, for on top of the general dearth of written materials on the subject of weaponless martial arts in Southeast Asia, sources dealing with Vietnam in particular are virtually non-existent. That such arts are presently being practiced is the only conclusive statement that can be made at the time of this writing.

Thailand

Thai kingdoms and Thai military ventures have for centuries played an instrumental role in the history of Southeast Asia. It was a warring Thai state that brought disaster to the Khmer Empire in 1432, and which, through the following centuries, dominated the area from Singapore to the Chinese border, and from the mouth of the Irrawaddy to the lower Mekong River.[14]

Numerous forms of unarmed combat are found in modern Thailand, of which the most famous—or notorious—art is simply called "Thai boxing." The emergence of this fighting technique into a sport is a recent development. Tourists as well as Thai citizens can be found thronging the many fighting arenas in and around the capital city of Bangkok. To the uninitiated, a Thai boxing contest first appears to be classically Western; the participants adorn themselves with the well-recognized boxing gloves and trunks, and square off in a roped fighting ring. However, those of us who are accustomed to "Marquis of Queensberry" rules are immediately shocked by the combatants' sudden lightning-like kicks to their opponents' torso or head, all of which is allowable conduct under Thai boxing rules.

These contests always begin with a rite or invocation that is so typically Indian that one almost expects to hear the chanting of verses from the *Ramayana* or to witness the execution of an Indian play. The combat itself is remindful of other Southeast Asian kicking styles and has prompted more than one writer to speculate that it was the precursor of Okinawan karate. Strangely enough, as we shall see later (Chapter Five), there is some merit to this assumption.

Thailand has been the sole Southeast Asian country to escape colonialism, either Western or Eastern. However, even without such direct rule, she displays many customs and traditions that bear unmistakable signs of both Indian and Chinese influence. So it is with her weaponless fighting arts which are, in many instances, indistinguishable from the Chinese and Indian. The chief reason for this strong Indo-Sino influence is that, in defeating and absorbing the Khmer Kingdom into its own culture, Thailand took unto itself all of the very strong Indian and Chinese cultural traits that therein lay.

Additionally, there has been a substantial "overseas" Chinese community of around two million living in Thailand for centuries. Though most are officially Thai citizens, these Chinese have preserved most of their ethnic practices, including social clubs and highly secretive military arts (i.e., *ch'üan fa*) associations. The latter are found in most of Thailand's larger cities, and have, for the most part, remained segregated in order to pre-serve their uniquely Chinese identity. On the other hand, small groups of native Thais through the years have managed to penetrate this "taboo" and learn many, if not all, of the secrets of the Chinese art.

Although there is a readily apparent *ch'üan fa* influ-ence in other Thai bare-handed combat techniques, it would be very difficult to determine what proportion is pure Thai art, and what proportion is *ch'üan fa*. Thus, from a popular standpoint Thai boxing remains the best rep-resentative of purely Thai weaponless martial arts.

Indonesia

The important role of geographical location in the development of a country's cultural patterns is particularly in evidence in those islands in Southeast Asia called Indo-nesia. Situated as it is on the trade route between China on the one hand and India, Western Asia, and Europe on the other, Indonesia has had great exposure to both Asian and European cultures.

The first inhabitants of the Indonesian archipelago are thought to have migrated both from mainland South-east Asia and from south China about 2000 B.C.[15] These peoples had just completed their stone-age cycle and were entering a bronze-age culture when, in the first century A.D., Hinduism and Buddhism made inroads into their civilization.[16] The strong effects of these two great religious systems are thought to have inspired the rapid rise of such empires as the Shrivijaya [SREE-vee-jai-ot] on the island of Sumatra, the Salendra dynasty of Java, and the Maja-pahit [MO-jo-pa-hcet] of East Java. Due largely to their borrowings from these well-established mainland cultures, Indonesia's empires flourished, and thus completely dominated the sociological development of all the member islands. Contact with India and China was maintained by each major Indonesian ruler in turn, and so these countries became the two great sources for Indonesia's weaponless martial art development.

There is insufficient historical evidence from which to infer with certainty which of these countries—India or China—gave Indonesia its first exposure to unarmed combat. And the situation is further complicated by the fact that Chinese, Arab, Malay, and Filipino pirates continually disrupted the rather sublime life of the Indonesians both at sea and among the coastal inhabitants. For many of the Indonesian natives, therefore, it was a matter of perfecting an effective fighting technique or being slaughtered.

In modern-day Indonesia four terms—*pukulan, pentjak, silat,* and *kun-tow*—are used to indicate unarmed combat in general, much like in the Western world we refer to essentially the same sport by the variant terms "boxing," "pugilism," "fisticuffs," etc. Speaking generally, *pukulan, pentjak, silat,* and *kun-tow* refer to variations of the same Indonesian art style that have developed in different geographical areas of the Indonesian archipelago. But technically, whenever one of the first three of the terms is used, reference is being made to a uniquely Indonesian development and is always written in the Bahasa Indonesian language, whereas the fourth term—*kun-tow* [k'unt'ou]—refers to a style or styles of Chinese *ch'üan fa* or *kung-fu,* and is written in Romanized Chinese.[17]

There are many, many variations on the general themes of *pukulan, pentjak,* and *silat* in contrast to the rela-

7. *Tji monjet* or "Ape Style."

8. *Tji kalong* or "Bat Style."

9. *Tji oelar* or "Snake Style."

6. The highest level of Indonesian *pukulan pentjak* is the *Kambangan*, or "Flower Dance," shown in the sequence of photographs and demonstrated by Paul De Thouars. A deceptively soft-looking *kata*, it is actually a combination of some of the most effective fighting movements. *Photographs by the author.*

tively few forms of Chinese *kun-tow*. The reason is that the Indonesian styles are localized in distinct areas, many being so specialized that they are considered to be the sole "property" of one village. Thus, while there is a proliferation of highly developed forms found in the islands, few inhabitants of Indonesia are able to avail themselves of instruction in more than one style. That style is generally representative of their home village or city, and as village rivalry is often intense, a master of one form of *pukulan, pentjak, silat,* or *kun-tow* would never teach his village's style to an outsider.

An exception to the above rule was found prior to Indonesia's independence from the Netherlands in 1949. Both native Indonesians and Dutch-Indonesians (or Eurasians as they are often called) who were in an upper-income class were able to avail themselves of the benefits of a Western education and consequently more profitable and prestigious positions in the Indonesian economy. Such people, therefore, lost their close village ties and could, if they sought out the proper "connections," learn various types of self-defense. Thus in more modern times we often find that the better-known masters are Dutch-Indonesian, some of whom even reside in Holland.

Because of the great number of village styles that developed, we will list only the more famous. When it is remembered that what is presently termed "Indonesia" encompasses an area but slightly smaller than the area of the United States and that many of the member islands of the archipelago have had little intercourse with the main islands of Sumatra, Java, Borneo, and Celebes, it is easier to see why such a disparity exists.

Common West Java types of *pukulan* include *tji bandar* [CHI BANDAR], a type of defense used by women and children, characterized by slight body movements and small steps of the feet, due largely to the tight fitting Indonesian sarong; *tji monjet* [CHI MOAN-yet] or "ape style"; *tji kalong* [CHI KAH-long] or "bat style"; *tji matjan* [CHI MAHT-jan] or "tiger style"; *tji mandih* [CHI MAHN-di], characterized by fluid, sweeping body movements; *tji oelar* [CHI OWE-lahr] or "snake style"; and *serak* [SEAR-awk] which invites attack by allowing an opponent to move close, then defeating him with superior speed and counter punching.[18]

In East Java the art is generally termed "pentjak." Here also is found a rather heavy settlement of permanent Chinese residents, such that *kun-tow* is another prominent East Javan form. The most significant *kun-tow* styles are: *minangkabau* [MEE-nang-kah-BAU] of Sumatra; *khilap* and *sjatung* [KEY-lahp and SHAN-tung] of Djakarta, capital city of Indonesia; *soetji hati* [SUIT-jee-HOT-ee] of Central Java; and *kontak* [KOHN-tahk] found primarily in West Java, that emphasizes punching of nerve centers.[19]

As previously observed, village rivalry is an integral part of Indonesia's culture. The most colorful way in which this is evidenced is in the pitting together of the various village champions during festivals held throughout the year. In each village a fighting champion is recognized who, because of his status as a fighting man, is called upon to represent his village's fighting style in combat. And, at the same time that he presents himself to defend his village honor, young men of his own village may challenge him if they feel they can defeat him. Thus if any of his fellow villagers defeats him, he steps down and a new champion is popularly heralded.

During the numerous holidays that the Indonesians celebrate, the high point of the festivities comes at the end of the day when a circular ring is formed outdoors for

10.   "Snake" versus "tiger"! This is the initial combat position taken during village competitions.

challenges to be met. Depending on the importance of the village holding such tourneys, fighting masters come out for these displays who are not normally seen at all during the balance of the year, and so it is exciting to everyone involved. Since training in his village's particular form of combat is a part of every young boy's education, there is not one of them who is not eager to see his village's chief protagonist pit his art against the others.

Actual combat takes place in the evening, the highlight of a long day of festive merriment. Torches are secured to long poles and planted in the ground in a circular pattern. As darkness approaches and the torches are lit, villagers anticipating the evening's entertainment begin congregating on the periphery of the illuminated circle, each hopeful that the local champion will emerge victorious.

Fighters from other localities move into the front rows

and wait to see the popular favorite. Drummers kneel to one side of the "arena," poised for the drama. With the entire village thus situated, the village champion and a female partner carrying a silken scarf enter the circle of light and begin the well-known *kambangan* [kahm-BAHNG-an] or flower dance. This is an uncannily graceful series of movements that demands the utmost physical conditioning in order to be properly executed. The throbbing drums bring the dance to its conclusion and the woman melts away into the crowd, leaving her scarf in the center of the ring.

This act of dropping the scarf signals the beginning of a fighting dance and also acts as the invitation for the fighters in the audience to try their combat skills with the figure in the circle. As the drumming tempo increases, the master performs the formal and stylized *langkas* and *djuroes* [JEW-rows], dancelike fighting movements that appear similar to the various karate *kata,* but which lack the stiff formality thereof. If the man's performance is flawless, the evening's entertainment might end at that point with no challengers risking defeat. If, on the other hand, the local master showed a weakness in his movements, a challenger invariably springs from the crowd and the battle begins in earnest. Interestingly enough, a foot-sweep causing an opponent to fall is oftentimes the margin of victory. If, however, the person knocked to the ground refuses to concede victory, a bloody contest will ensue in which death is not uncommon for one of the combatants. The foot-sweeping technique is still generally the basis for victory in these formal competitions, and as odd as this may seem on first thought, it becomes obvious that this is supremely logical, since at the level of adroitness that these men find themselves, where a hundredth of a second of timing becomes all-important, any man who is sufficiently superior to his opponent to upset him with a foot-sweep will invariably be superior in actual combat.

Malaya

The Malay Peninsula extends down through the heart of Southeast Asia, acting as a bridge to Indonesia and the islands of the western Pacific. Malayan peoples share with other Southeast Asians a widespread religious and cultural heritage from India. It is also very likely that India influenced the development of a weaponless system of fighting called *bersilat* [bur-SEE-lot]; however, there is more direct evidence at the present time to enforce the common hypothesis that China was the real spiritual force behind *bersilat*'s evolvement in Malaya.

Bersilat in translation means "self-defense," but according to a popular legend its origin is said to have been based on a woman named "Bersilat" who, through a series of dreams, acquired a knowledge of the fundamentals of empty-handed fighting.[20] Other than this legend, there is very little written materials to be found giving the history of the art.

Malayan weddings and other festive occasions are almost always highlighted by *bersilat* exhibitions, and in some instances actual fighting contests can even be seen as part of the entertainment.[21] *Bersilat* exists today in two forms: One, *silat pulat,* is purely for public display and exhibition, while the other form, called *silat buah,* is used in actual combat.[22]

Exhibition *bersilat* is probably the more graceful of the two forms. It is greatly stylized and artificial in its exe-

11. The importance of *bersilat,* a primary Malayan art form, is evidenced by the recent issuance of a postage stamp depicting the art.

cution, having as its base a system of conventional gestures and movements which are entirely prearranged. Again, like its Indonesian counterparts (i.e. *pukulan, pentjak, silat,* and *kun-tow*), musical and rhythmic accompaniment are used for *bersilat* in exhibition.

The deadly *silat buah* is generally practiced in semiseclusion. Here, the secret moves are passed on from master to disciple under a vow of secrecy,[23] reminiscent of Chinese *ch'üan fa.* Various forms of *silat buah* can be found throughout the narrow peninsula of Malaysia, but the most popular forms are fist and finger attacking, grappling and defeating an opponent by using locks, throws, and various grips, and a spectacular style which utilizes high leaps and flying kicks.

Bersilat varies from state to state in Malaysia, and indeed from teacher to teacher, but the east coast of Malaya is generally considered to have the best men of the art. *Kun-tow* is also practiced in the larger cities where numerous Chinese clubs exist, and where a rivalry between *kun-tow* associations and *bersilat* groups exists. Little information is known about the resulting clashes that occur between these rival factions.

With the passing of the war years—both world and civil—and the use of the *kris* as the basic means for fighting, and with a more readily disciplined and law abiding citizenry, *bersilat* as a secret art of combat is slowly giving way to *bersilat* as a sport and means of physical exercise.[24]

A tape recorded interview at the University of Malaya, with *bersilat* expert Abdul Samat, was conducted by Dr. B. C. Stone and Dr. G. B. Evans:

DR. STONE: What does *bersilat* mean in English?

MR. SAMAT: In English, *bersilat* means "self-defense." The name "bersilat" itself comes from a woman's name—"Bersilat." She is said to have learned the various forms of unarmed combat in her sleep.

DR. STONE: In other words she learned the techniques of self-defense in a dream?

MR. SAMAT: Yes.

DR. STONE: Did *bersilat* originate in Malaya?

MR. SAMAT: No, it originated in Sumatra.

DR. STONE: How long ago was this?

MR. SAMAT: In 1511.

DR. STONE: Did the Malayans or the Sumatrans have a soldier or military class such as the Indian *Kshátriya* or the Japanese *samurai?* If so, did they practice *bersilat?*

MR. SAMAT: In Sumatra, I do not know, but here they have a military caste that is trained in *bersilat.*

DR. STONE: What do they call these soldiers?

MR. SAMAT: *Ten-tera* or Royal Army.

DR. STONE: Would these soldiers be attached to the court of a sultan?

MR. SAMAT: Yes. Each tribe and each village in Malaya has leaders who group their men into local armies. When the sultan of a district needs men to fight a war, he tells his village leaders to call upon their men.

DR. STONE: Has there been any Chinese influence in *bersilat?*

MR. SAMAT: Lately there has been Chinese influence.

DR. STONE: You mean that Chinese influence on the development of *bersilat* is a modern development?

MR. SAMAT: Yes, especially the Peking style of *kuntow*. We have not had Peking style before. Prior to this influence, kicking with the leg was considered very rude. This would be for exhibition style only, of course; in real self-defense any part of the body could be used.

DR. STONE: Then the Chinese influence would be found only in the real fighting and not in the exhibition category of *bersilat?*

MR. SAMAT: Yes.

DR. STONE: Would you say the exhibition form of *bersilat* is the closest thing to the old forms of *bersilat?*

MR. SAMAT: Yes, this form follows the old culture.

DR. STONE: In karate and *kung-fu,* there are certain movement exercises. In *bersilat,* do students learn such movements utilizing the attacking aspects of the art? In other words, do students learn certain dance-like movements and definite sequences having a specific name?

MR. SAMAT: No, each movement does not have a distinct name, but the student has to learn the movements step-by-step. The first movement in *bersilat* is to learn the "break-fall" [breaking one's fall like in judo exercises], and then the student goes on learning each movement up to a total of forty-four.

DR. STONE: If you were actually in a fight, would you change the sequence of these steps?

MR. SAMAT: In a real fight you would normally use whatever movements are the most convenient to you.

DR. STONE: Then one would have to have a complete memory of all the steps and be able to pick out instantly the one form or forms you would use?

MR. SAMAT: Yes. You must always have an eye on the enemy, and especially the head and shoulders.

DR. STONE: Why is this?

MR. SAMAT: Because if the enemy wants to kick you, his head moves. If he wants to spear you with a weapon or punch you, the shoulders move. These are the keys.

DR. STONE: What parts of the body are used as weapons in *bersilat?*

MR. SAMAT: The heel of the palm, the little finger and the side of the palm, the elbow, the shoulder, the knee, the balls of the feet, the heel of the foot, and your head, too.

DR. STONE: Do you have ways of training these various parts of the body making them tougher?

MR. SAMAT: Oh yes!

DR. STONE: How do you train, by punching things?

MR. SAMAT: The usual thing is to put sand into a sack of some sort and punch this every day. Later on, punching trees of a certain variety hardens the knuckles. This takes at least forty-four days and one cannot stop it even for a single day, or if one's hand bleeds from the pounding.

DR. STONE: Would a *bersilat* student usually choose a tree that had a smooth bark?

MR. SAMAT: Usually, any convenient tree is chosen.

DR. EVANS: What type of tree do you use?

MR. SAMAT: I use the Jack Fruit tree, and, normally, you are expected to practice this punching until the tree dies.

DR. STONE: Do you have stunts or demonstrations, such as breaking pieces of wood or bricks, or something of that nature?

MR. SAMAT: We do not have this practice in *bersilat,* but we could break these things.

DR. EVANS: Do you ever practice striking bamboo?

MR. SAMAT: No, this is too dangerous because bamboo cuts you very easily.

DR. STONE: Moving on to another area. Are there national or local competitions in *bersilat?* Would you have a national or local champion?

MR. SAMAT: Yes, they have such things nowadays.

DR. STONE: Is there one for each state?

MR. SAMAT: Contests are held at local festivals and celebrations.

DR. STONE: How often do they hold these competitions?

MR. SAMAT: Usually, once a year.

DR. EVANS: Is it stopped now? I understood they stopped having the contests since last year [1965].

DR. STONE: Why is that?

MR. SAMAT: I really do not know, but maybe the funds for these competitions are gone.

DR. STONE: Does this mean that fewer people are studying *bersilat* now?

MR. SAMAT: There are actually more people studying *bersilat* now.

DR. STONE: But they have ended the championships now?

MR. SAMAT: Yes.

DR. STONE: What does the government think about *bersilat?* Is it government supported?

MR. SAMAT: There seems to be no official government position concerning the art.

DR. STONE: Do you know of any influence from other Southeast Asian countries?

MR. SAMAT: I do not know.

DR. EVANS: When you were trained, were there other students present?

MR. SAMAT: There were three of us.

DR. EVANS: Did you practice the movement steps together?

MR. SAMAT: No, some students take longer to pass each step.

DR. STONE: Describe the colors of the costume you wear in *bersilat*.

MR. SAMAT: In the beginning the costume is white, and the second step the dress is black. The third step has a black, white, and red costume. That is, white trousers and shirt, black sash, and a red jacket. An instructor wears all green.

DR. EVANS: What about the headdress?

MR. SAMAT: The headdress is normally red for all those who complete the final step. When you become an assistant instructor you wear a green one.

DR. EVANS: Have you done any instructing?

MR. SAMAT: Yes I have.

DR. STONE: Have you studied other styles of *bersilat?*

MR. SAMAT: Not styles, but types. One from Java, and the *minangkabau* form from Sumatra.

DR. STONE: How do these types differ from *bersilat?*

MR. SAMAT: They have different steps and different movements.

DR. STONE: Is one supposed to be better than another?

MR. SAMAT: Well, I find the *sjatung* form quite good. Better even than the *minangkabau* and other Javanese forms.

DR. STONE: How many types or styles are there?

MR. SAMAT: We have in Malaya the Javanese *silat,* the Sumatran *minangkabau,* the *bayan silat,* the *sjatung silat,* and the *kontak silat.* This last form is very dangerous because it attacks the nerve centers.

DR. EVANS: You mean they strike the sensitive areas of the body?

MR. SAMAT: Yes, they usually chop these places.

DR. EVANS: In *bersilat,* I believe they use no weapons. Is this correct?

MR. SAMAT: No, in *bersilat* they use a short stick, club, or actually anything. In Malaya the *kris* [knife] is often used. The use of certain knives is an Islamic influence. There is also some Arabic influence in some of the steps.

DR. EVANS: When you strike do you make a noise?

MR. SAMAT: Yes, to frighten the enemy.

DR. EVANS: Do you learn distraction methods to fool your opponent?

MR. SAMAT: Yes, this is done. There are many of these techniques.

DR. EVANS: Did you learn any of these feinting methods?

MR. SAMAT: These are learned only by attackers, so I did not learn them.

DR. EVANS: When you are using *bersilat* in combat do you watch an opponent's eyes as well as his head and shoulders?

MR. SAMAT: Yes, all parts of the head.

DR. EVANS: Do you watch his legs as well?

MR. SAMAT: No. When the leg moves the head will also move. If the head does not move the strike will lack power and not hurt you.

DR. STONE: Has the training of *bersilat* ever been written down?

MR. SAMAT: As far as I know it has not been written down.

DR. STONE: Then you would say one learns this art

by personal communication with the instructor?

MR. SAMAT: Yes. It is very difficult to describe each step.

DR. EVANS: What did you find to be the hardest thing to learn in your *bersilat* training?

MR. SAMAT: The break-fall is the hardest.

Bersilat today remains one of the very rare fighting arts of the world due to the intense secrecy with which it evolved in Malaya. So little has been written about the art that few *ch'üan fa* and karate experts know anything of *bersilat* or Malayan fighting arts in general. Those persons interested in this esoteric Southeast Asian martial art can find more information in articles published in the *Journal of the Straits Malayan Branch Royal Asiatic Society* over the last fifty years. Exact data can be found in the "Bibliography of Malaya," edited in two volumes by Cheeseman and Beda Lim, *JMBRAS* of 1960 and 1961.[25]

Chapter 5

Okinawa

OKINAWA was generally absent from the mainstream of world history until 1945 when it served as the scene for the epic showdown battle between the two military giants of the Pacific Ocean, Japan and the American Allied forces. This sequestered island, however, has been the site of many an intrigue between Japan and China, and has itself, at one time or another, been embroiled in life-and-death power struggles with both of these great Asian political rivals.

"Okinawa," the principal island of the Ryukyu archipelago, means "a rope in the offing."[1] An apt description indeed, seeing that this long slender island lies near the center of a line of islands that stretch from Japan in the north to the very doorstep of China in the south. The prevailing winds and the Japan Current sweep away from continental Asia, close to the Ryukyus, and on past Japan into the North Pacific. Okinawa was truly a "rope in the offing" for those unfortunate mainland sailors who found themselves forced out into the open sea with no apparent rescue at hand. We shall see these shipwrecked castaways to be an integral part of our story.

The southernmost island of the Ryukyu chain is visible from the island of Taiwan, now the site of Chiang Kai-shek's Nationalist Chinese government. The northernmost island over seven hundred miles away lies within miles of Kyushu, the southernmost of Japan's four major islands.[2] Between these extremities are one hundred-forty islands, only thirty-six of which are permanently settled.[3]

The origin of the Okinawan people is one of those fascinating anthropological mysteries. There are strong indications that Okinawa's first inhabitants were the survivors of an ancient shipwreck, the chance result of one of the vicious typhoons for which the area is noted. If such is the case, historians will forever be deprived of the valuable written materials usually found in connection with the volitional movement and migration of peoples. If, on the other hand, man reached the Ryukyus in Paleolithic or neolithic times, as some evidence suggests, written materials would again be virtually non-existent.

Besides our hypothetical castaways who depended for survival upon what they could forage from the countryside, there were occasional immigrations of peoples from the north who brought with them household belongings, domestic animals, tools, and religious items. It appears that these immigrations were quite infrequent, and that there have been no new immigrations into Okinawa of any consequence within the last two thousand years.[4] Thus the general patterns of Ryukyuan culture were established over two millennia ago.

The physiognomy of the Okinawans more closely resembles the Japanese than any other Asian people. However, many Okinawans are found with Southeast Asian physical characteristics, thus indicating a strong strain of Malayo-Polynesian blood. There is a very positive Southeast Asian influence on the architecture of the Ryukyuan chain, and there are a number of linguistic similarities, although the language forms throughout the Ryukyus have a much stronger affinity with archaic Japanese. We know that there were Ryukyuan contacts with the Asian continent as early as the third century B.C., a fact that is shown by the number of artifacts identified with north China that have been found near Naha, the present capital of Okinawa.[5] The inevitable conclusion, then, is that there were cultural influences that found their way into the Ryukyu Islands from the east, from the north, and from the south,[6] and that "Okinawan culture" is a blending of these elements.

For our purposes, the significance of these findings lies only in the fact that sometime, from one or more of these three outside areas, there came an influx of weaponless fighting techniques that were the progenitors of modern-day karate. As we saw earlier, China saw the development of the Shaolin *ch'üan fa* by the Indian monk Bodhidharma in the sixth century, and, though there may have been some kind of weaponless fighting as early as the third century B.C., it did not develop into an organized system of unarmed self-defense until after Bodhidharma's advent.

China's earliest planned contact with the Ryukyus came during the Sui dynasty (A.D. 580–618). This period was one of intellectual intrigue instigated by Emperor Yang Chien's attempts to find the secrets of eternal life and a means of turning base metals into gold.[7] Yang Chien outfitted a number of expeditions to "barbarian" lands in his search for the legendary "Land of Happy Immortals" to the east.[8] During one of these forays in the seventh century (*ca.* A.D. 608) a number of islands were found in the eastern seas. But the inhabitants were far from being "Happy Immortals." This we know from later reports by the expedition's commander, in which it was related that many of the inhabitants of one specific island lost their lives during the ensuing skirmish with Chinese marines of the expeditionary force. Although the exact location of the islands which were the subject of this report was never factually determined, various authorities have taken the stand that they were in the Ryukyu group, and that the besieged island was probably Okinawa. This deduction is based in large part upon the fact that soon after Emperor Yang Chien's rule Chinese documents began referring to all of the islands between Japan and the Philippines as "Liu Ch'iu," using the ideographs that are pronounced in Japanese as "Ryukyu"[9] [rhee-you-cue].

By the seventh century, China had officially recognized Japan as an independent political entity. At various times official diplomatic and cultural missions comprised of Japanese priests, soldiers, and statesmen, passed between the Chinese mainland and Japan. A few of these missions were reported missing, with no explanation as to why. We can only surmise that the immediate cause for such disappearances was shipwreck, and that the survivors became inhabitants of islands out of the mainstream of diplomatic travel. What specific influence these survivors had on the development of primitive Ryukyuan culture is not precisely known, but educated speculation leads us to believe that it was far reaching.

Did these travelers bring a karate-like art to Okinawa? This theory is plausible, as members of the Japanese warrior class or samurai generally escorted these missions. Also, peripatetic Buddhist priests and scholars commuted regularly between Japan and China in the seventh and eighth centuries, and we have seen (Chapter Two) that such individuals were often deft proponents of unarmed self-defense techniques. Japanese students of Buddhism studying in Chinese monasteries were undoubtedly exposed to the Shaolin techniques of the monk Bodhidharma, and it is reported that many of the more adventurous of these, after completing their training, set sail to the eastward in order to spread the teachings to the known world. Such monks, if stranded on a distant island in the Ryukyus, would doubtlessly have introduced the natives to their form of self-defense as well as to their religion. But again, there is no concrete proof of such occurrences, and so such possibilities must remain in the realm of conjecture.

There is a widely held hypothesis that *ch'üan fa* entered the Ryukyus via China's Foochow district during the sixth- and seventh-century reign of China's Sui dynasty.[10] Such Chinese-Ryukyuan contacts are first mentioned in the section on "Eastern Barbarians" of the *Sui Shu,* the dynastic history of the Sui rulers.[11] Then again, the definitive Japanese encyclopedia, *Sekai Dai-Hyakka-jiten,* states that karate or a type of *ch'üan fa* was probably brought to Okinawa from China during the T'ang dynasty (A.D. 618–906).[12]

Possibly the strongest support for the claim that karate is an innate part of Okinawan culture is based on some of the Ryukyu islanders' classical dances. The parts danced by males during certain festivals resemble modern karate movements. Add to this the fact that these festivals have been performed since earliest recorded history, and there seems to be a fair case for Okinawan dancing being a precursor to karate.[13] But, as we cannot tell where these dances came from, it may be concluded that Chinese influence on Okinawan weaponless combat did not occur until later in the 14th century.

From the end of the T'ang dynasty to the beginning of the Ming period in 1368—a span of 450 years—there is an unexplained silence regarding the development of karate in the Ryukyus. Not only is there a dearth of written materials on the subject, but even oral traditions concerning the art are vague and generally lacking. Certainly, had *ch'üan fa* been introduced to Okinawa between the Sui and Ming periods—nearly 800 years—and found acceptance in the Ryukyuan culture, evidence of it would be readily locatable in Ryukyuan cultural annals.

In 1372 official Chinese-Okinawan relations were instituted when Okinawa's King Satto expressed his allegiance to the Ming Emperor of China. In so doing, the Okinawan king not only relegated his domain to tributary status, but also threw open Okinawa's watery doors to greatly intensified Chinese cultural influence.[14] With Okinawa now a Chinese satellite, a cultural proselytization began in earnest. In the following centuries *ch'üan fa* found its way into the Ryukyus thus aiding the establishment of a regular system of unarmed self-defense, based partly on the indigenous Okinawan form of fighting with fists.

This ancient Okinawan style of combat is termed *tode* [toe-day]. Many Japanese historians and Okinawan karate masters feel that in spite of the lack of supportive evidence, this art is native to the Ryukyu Islands, and that when *tode* was combined with other fighting styles introduced from Asia, the art of karate evolved. Therefore, among the Orientalists who have studied Okinawan military history and martial art development, there is a general agreement that *ch'üan fa* is only partly responsible for the birth of present-day Okinawan karate. (The author concurs with this assumption only to the point that the closed fist technique of modern karate, because of its long use in the Ryukyus as a primary means of wartime survival and its resulting emphasis on maiming and killing, is "native" to the Ryukyus, though he feels that it had its ultimate beginning in the Chinese art of *ch'üan fa.*)

The oral transmission of historical events is often more reliable than written records. In Okinawa, since little recorded data has been found on the history of karate, we look to the oral traditions which cite the beginning of the 14th century as the period when a karate-like art began to be practiced generally. This budding art was greatly stimulated by the large mission of Chinese officials and their entourage, sent to Okinawa by Emperor Hung Wu-ti in 1372. Needless to say, the exponents of *ch'üan fa* on this excursion made a positive impression on interested Okinawans.

In the Ming period (1368–1644) a permanent Okinawan settlement began to develop on Chinese soil at the Chinese capital of Ch'uan-chou. In terms of lasting Chinese influence upon Okinawan history, this settlement was extremely important; for not only did commuting Okinawan citizens bring back to their islands artifacts and customs, but they brought a general belief that all things Chinese were indeed superior.[15] Although in a historical sense Chinese influence was slow in reaching the more remote areas of the Ryukyus, it did, in time, penetrate to even the most isolated islands so that the blending of cultures was eventually complete. These firm cultural ties were to last for five hundred years.[16]

The year 1393 saw a sudden spurt in the migration of Chinese people to Okinawa. This was the result of an imperial gift from China in the form of a large body of skilled artisans and merchants.[17] This group of Chinese, which soon had formed into its own community, has long been referred to as the "Thirty-six Families." Such numeration of people with a homogeneity of purpose has been common in Chinese society. Yet in this case the term refers to a much larger number; i.e., to Okinawa's Chinese community as a whole. Oral tradition states that these "Thirty-six Families" were largely responsible for the spread of *ch'üan fa* throughout the Ryukyu Islands.[18]

In 1429 Okinawa became a unified kingdom under the dynamic leadership of a man named Hashi. Hashi, following the ages-old Chinese and Japanese practice of "rule from the wings," appointed his father King of Chuzan, since Chuzan was at that time the most important of the three Okinawan principalities of Chuzan, Hokuzan, and Nanzan.[19] Shortly after acquiring control of the land, Hashi renamed these principalities, changing Chuzan to Nakagami, Hokuzan to Kunigami, and Nanzan to Shimajiri.[20]

Okinawa at first profited little from this unification, as the peasants and quasi-nobility, called *anji,* still lived for the most part at the same bare subsistence level as that of their ancestors. But this was soon to change. Because of his exposure to Chinese government officials and a knowledge of Okinawa's isolated position, Hashi learned a great deal about improving economic conditions in his country. One of his first lessons involved the great importance of active trade relations with other countries. Since Ryukyuans had long been able seafarers, they quite naturally fell into their newly appointed roles as commercial sea traders.[21] Thus for the following two centuries Okinawa's two large towns, Shuri and Naha, became famous as centers of an increasingly profitable traffic in luxury goods, since wares purchased in the Indies and the bazaars of Southeast Asia were brought to Okinawa and reshipped to China, Korea, and Japan.[22]

The effect of this extensive trade on the development of karate is readily apparent when it is realized that Okinawans were suddenly, as it were, having widespread contact with those Arabs, Malays, Indonesians, and Thai who frequented the centers of commerce. Of course, such contact in itself is not enough to assure us of an exchange of ideas on weaponless fighting systems. But when we add two ingredients, bored and lonely seamen, and free-flowing spirits, we suddenly have a stage set for a great deal of volatile cultural interaction. In Chapter Four we already established the fact that karate-like arts were well developed in Indonesia (Indies), Malaya, Thailand, and other seaport islands in the South China Sea. We therefore arrive at a picture of brawling sailors performing a very picturesque, although undoubtedly bloody, exchange of "ideas" on weaponless fighting techniques. It is a virtual certainty that at this time Okinawans gained most, if not all, of their insight into the Southeast Asian forms of unarmed combat, which fact is stated unequivocally by the acknowledged authority on Okinawan history, George H. Kerr.[23]

Records in Okinawa's national archives that were, unfortunately, destroyed during World War II, indicated that between 1432 and 1570 Okinawa established forty-four official embassies in Annam (Vietnam), Thailand, Malaya, and many of the lesser kingdoms of Java.[24] This intercourse is particularly meaningful to us, since it helps to verify a long-held conviction that modern karate kicking techniques were imported from the area known until quite recently as Indochina,[25] (i.e., Vietnam,

Cambodia, and Laos), whereas the open-handed and finger-stabbing techniques in offensive karate movements evolved from different locations.

Probably the single most important date in Okinawan history is 1609. The great Satsuma clan in southern Kyushu (Japan), led by the Shimazu family, had been on the losing side in the Japanese civil war of 1600. The victorious Tokugawa clan, as was customary in Japan, allowed the Satsuma clan to retain its feudal territories as a *tozama daimyo* (outside lord). However, because of the potential threat that all such *tozama* rulerships held for the victorious faction, close government scrutiny was kept over the Satsuma samurai. Then, by Tokugawa decree, Satsuma was "permitted" to march against the Ryukyu Islands. This was done both to punish Okinawa for refusing to supply Japan with materials needed for her abortive attack on China in 1592, and because the Tokugawa *shogun* (generalissimo) feared the armed strength of Satsuma and felt that an overseas "adventure" would be the perfect prescription for soothing the frustrations of Shimazu's warriors.[26] The resulting military expedition in 1609 ended Okinawan independence and made way for complete Satsuma control over all the Ryukyus.

A number of prohibitive ordinances proclaimed by Iehisa Shimazu included a ban on all weapons. Arms found in an Okinawan's possession were immediately confiscated and the owner or holder thereof severely punished. The bitterness that arose from such total subjugation was difficult for many of the islanders to bear in silence, and clashes between the two factions began to occur. In such battles the Okinawans were forced to use the only "weapons" they still possessed, which generally amounted to little more than their bare hands and feet.[27]

Seeing that such disunited resistance was gaining them little, the various Okinawan *ch'üan fa* groups and *tode* societies had a series of secret conferences which resulted in their banding together in 1629 as a united front against the enemy. The result was that a new fighting style developed from this combination of *tode* and *ch'üan fa,* which was simply called *te* and translated "hand."[28] This 17th-century development is the first recorded instance of an art that closely approximates modern karate. *Te* might be described as the intermediate stage between *tode-ch'üan fa* and karate.

During these early years of development, *te* practice was shrouded in the utmost secrecy due to the iron-clad Satsuma edict that was designed to eradicate every trace of the Okinawan martial arts.[29] The three leading *te* schools—located in Shuri, Naha, and Tomari—went "underground" to avoid detection by the Satsuma samurai. Because of this turn of events, *te* took on two distinctive characteristics: first, it became known as an esoteric art because of the secrecy under which it was taught and practiced; second, it became extremely violent since the sole purpose of its practitioners was to maim or kill. Historically speaking, this going underground had the effect of halting the written chroniclization of the art, and for the next century or so we must again rely on oral traditions. The best verified of these traditions come to us in the form of legends.

One of these legends states that a certain man named Sakugawa from Shuri made a trip to China in 1724 in quest of initiation into the *ch'üan fa* arts. As he was not heard from for many years, his kin thought him lost. But one day, many years later, he reappeared in Shuri, a greatly changed man. His apparent mastery over his body, and the skill with which he performed the extremely complex *ch'üan fa kata* (dancelike movements), caused many to ask to become his pupils. The result was the now-famed Sakugawa School of karate which, though termed a "karate school" by the famous Okinawan karate master Gichin Funakoshi,[30] was probably based on pure Chinese *ch'üan fa*.

The second legend important for our purposes is based on another Shuri resident named Shionja. Together with a Chinese friend, Kushanku (Japanese pronunciation) with whom he had studied *ch'üan fa* in China, he returned to his home on Okinawa in 1784 after residence abroad. The many disciples who accompanied the pair helped to popularize yet another style of *ch'üan fa*. This incident is recorded in a book entitled *Oshima Hikki* whose author, a certain Tobe of Tosa village, is said to have obtained the story in detail through a series of interviews with Shionja himself.[31] Aside from these two tales there is little of any consequence about karate development in even the oral chronology until 1903 when this art was first publicly demonstrated on Okinawa.[32]

Between 1784 and 1903 "karate" replaced "te" as the term commonly used to designate the major form of Okinawan weaponless fighting. Of course, there were those who preferred using the antiquated terms "te" and "tode," and who have persisted in so doing into the present day. Some writers have even stated that the term "karate" was not known until 1902 or 1903.[33] However, upon interviewing Okinawan immigrants in Hawaii a karate practitioner was found who had studied karate as a youth in Okinawa as early as 1894, and who knew the art to be called "karate" at that time.[34] Thus, although it is not possible to point with certainty to the time when this term became common in Okinawa, the evidence available indicates that it took place in the latter part of the 19th century.

In 1904 karate, written 唐手, was officially introduced into the Okinawan public schools as a regular part of the physical education curriculum.[35] "Karate" thus became a more or less standard term by 1910 and remained so until the "new" ideographs 空手 (see Chapter One) replaced the old in approximately 1936.

*   *   *   *

It has been almost impossible to tell when the secrecy surrounding karate was relaxed. Several modern karate authorities claim that the intense seclusion of karate was maintained until about 1903.[36] This supposition seems difficult to believe in view of the fact that in 1875 Satsuma's "unofficial" occupation of Okinawa ended and the Ryukyu Islands became officially a part of the Japanese Empire. With Japan's recognition of Okinawa as part of the nation, so to speak, the Okinawan people would seemingly have no further reason for retaining such secrecy. But logic and reality do not always coincide.

One explanation is the fact that secret societies of any type find it difficult to suddenly change their traditional character. Another explanation lies in the intense rivalry that developed within the karate schools of Naha, Shuri, and Tomari. This rivalry was the result of the all-too-human failing of not being able to adjust to peace after an intense period of war. Since the practitioners of these arts had been trained primarily to kill, they were suddenly faced with a lack of enemies. And so each school began vying with the others for supremacy in these arts.[37]

In most cases, the leaders of the schools did their best

12. Two scenes from Toho Studios' famous "Judo Saga" in which a typically black-garbed karate villain assaults a judoist, hero of the story and the ultimate victor. *Courtesy of Toho International.*

to keep the rivalry on the plane of a competitive sport with the goal of teaching pupils to administer quasi-death-dealing blows to one another which were stopped in mid-air a split second before the lethal physical contact was made. On the other hand, many of the Okinawan schools preferred to keep their art on a higher level, disdaining from competitions of any sort and practicing only the *kata* movements as the sole means for mastery of their particular style. A few of the present-day Okinawan masters refuse to be swept-up in the sporting elements possible in karate, thus *dan* (grade) ranking, tournaments, or even practice sparring matches within the circle of students is prohibited. In the clubs where competitions became a featured part of training there were naturally many accidents before a set of iron-clad rules was worked out, and many hot-tempered individuals failed completely to heed the "new wave" of non-violence. The unfortunate result was that some karate adherents became labeled as generally unsavory. This tradition has carried through to the present day where, in most Japanese films in which an exponent of karate is depicted, he is invariably portrayed as a villain. Because of these characteristics of karate development, those applying for their admission to a karate school were generally called upon to take rather severe vows of silence and allegiance. This was done so that they would realize the importance of preventing at all cost the secrets they were about to learn from leaking into a rival camp. It is interesting to note that similar precautions have been taken in various Hawaiian karate clubs in recent years.

We have seen that karate development on Okinawa was limited in scope and popular appeal before 1903. Oral records are responsible for many of the myths and theories of karate development. Since there are virtually no written references to the native art of the Ryukyus *(tode)*, the scant information that we have on it is based on oral traditions as well. However, by exploring briefly the development of the ideographs standing for the various art forms associated with karate or its prototypes, we can see some very interesting, tangible, occurrences.

Tode is considered indigenous to Okinawa because *ch'üan fa* uses mainly *kaishu* 開手, which refers to open-handed techniques, while *tode* employs the use of the fist technique called *taiso* 太祖.[38] *Taiso* literally means "founder" or "progenitor" and the same characters are sometimes used to represent the founder of the T'ang dynasty (A.D. 618–906) in China. Why a set of ideographs having so much Chinese association would be used to represent the closed-fist style, which is thought to be native to Okinawa, is a mystery. A possible explanation can be found in Okinawa's long time role of subservience to China. Until the Satsuma invasion in 1609 there was a constant and influential clique of pro-Chinese advisers to the various Okinawan kings, and Okinawa continued to pay tribute to China even after formal annexation by Japan. It is no wonder that many so-called Okinawan customs have a Chinese "flavor." Linguistically, it is possible that the *tode* [toe-day] pronunciation of the ideographs 唐手 was in existence before *ch'üan fa* played a major role in the culmination of modern karate and that when the Chinese writing system was established on Okinawa, the Chinese ideographs that phonetically approximated "tode" were written 唐手.

There seems to be a general agreement among contemporary karate authorities that Chinese *ch'üan fa* did play an important part in the development of this fight-

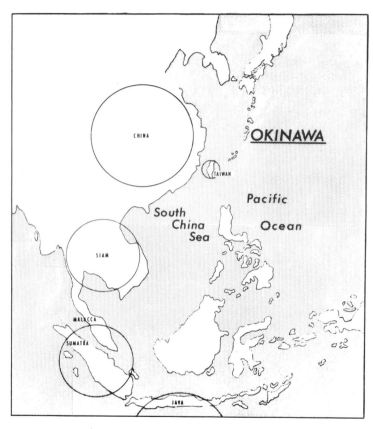

13.   Map of East & Southeast Asia with circled areas indicating the geographical sources of Okinawan karate.

ing art so closely associated with the Ryukyu Islands. Modern karate is said to be a combination of closed-fist techniques from Okinawa, ends-of-the-finger *(nukite)* techniques from Taiwan, open-handed forms from China, and kicking techniques from Southeast Asia.[39]

It was previously explained how the Chinese-Ryukyu Island intercourse developed; however, the routes that the Taiwanese elements of karate took in their migration to Okinawa are not definitely established. Due to the proximity of Taiwan it is possible that direct communication between these two areas resulted in Okinawan adaption of the Taiwan finger-stab. As we saw earlier, there were numerous exchanges between Okinawa, Thailand, and Indochina. Kicking arts may have come direct from Thailand or Indochina or entered the Ryukyu Islands indirectly via Taiwan or Foochow in China.

By way of a summary, karate development in Okinawa can be broken into rather well-defined periods. There was a form of weaponless martial art between A.D. 580–906, which corresponds to the Sui and T'ang periods in China; however, the information concerning these eras is scanty and lacking in definitive resource material. From 906 to 1300 there is little information regarding any form of fighting styles. Between 1300 and 1570, which roughly corresponds to the Ming dynasty in China, we find oral traditions concerning *ch'üan fa* and *tode* activity in Okinawa. During the secretive years (1609 to 1903) we find little information of karate activity, although this was the period of the greatest karate development.

After 1903 karate became more or less standardized in various styles or "ryu," some of which are: *Goju-ryu, Shorin-ryu, Shotokan-ryu, Nihon Kempo-ryu, Shindo Jinen-ryu, Wado-ryu, Kushin-ryu,* and *Kan-ryu.*[40]

14.   A profusion of Okinawan postage stamps with karate themes indicates its prominence. Three are shown here.

In 1915 karate was brought into Japan by Gichin Funakoshi when he demonstrated the art at the great Japanese martial arts headquarters in Kyoto called the Butoku-den.[41] During the years following 1915 a number of other famous Okinawan karate masters journeyed to Japan to teach their art, thus formally informing the world abroad that it, too, was deserving of being added to the list of progenitors of an effective and well-developed system of weaponless hand-to-hand combat.

Chapter 6

Japan

"THINGS Japanese" have been much in vogue in the two decades since the end of World War II. And yet, Japanese history and traditions are still but superficially understood in the West, in spite of the great amount of *bavardage* written by so-called "experts" interested more in financial return than in authenticated truth.

Books dealing with *bu-jutsu* (Japanese martial arts in general) have, particularly in the past few years, glutted the world's "Orientalist" markets. Too many, however, have been written by those who lack the credentials for authorship or who have failed to compile sufficient *apparatus criticus* to support their works. Karate, specifically, has been badly misrepresented because of the innumerable attempts to acquaint the American public with it in the form of a "how-to" sport, or as a means of protecting oneself against the bullies of life. The effect of all this sensationalistic journalism has been that the average reader is pretty well convinced not only that karate was designed primarily as a lethal way of disposing of one's enemies, but also that in its origins it is as Japanese as Shinto, Mt. Fuji, and cherry blossoms.

Japan, though not the birthplace of karate, has had, since hoary antiquity, a tradition of rather exotic military arts. In practice, some of these have an admitted resemblance to modern karate. In Japan's mythological era (before A.D. 500) it is said that the demi-gods Takeminakatano Kami and Takemikazuchino Kami engaged in some sort of hand-to-hand combat which the records refer to as a "strength contest."[1] From the depictions of this historical battle, we can infer that they were pitting one weaponless fighting art against another. During this same dawning period of the historical age, another legendary duel occurred between Nomi-No Sukune and Taemonokehaya,[2] again with no weapons. References to such contests abound in Japan's early literature dealing with the birth of a unified Japanese nation, and although these tales are couched in the symbolism of Japanese mythology, there is every likelihood that many, if not all, were inspired by actual struggles.

A few writers have deduced a positive similarity between these contests and judo (of ju-jutsu, or incorrectly, jiu-jitsu) and *sumo* wrestling. However, closer scrutiny indicates that the type of fighting depicted more nearly resembles what is currently lumped together under the heading of karate. But at this point great care in drawing conclusions must be exercised. We are by no means implying that karate per se so existed in ancient Japan. The system of movements called karate is, as we have seen, an eclectic art that reached its culmination in the Ryukyu Islands. The possibility does exist, however, that a type of *ch'üan fa* found its way into early Japan and that it was instrumental in the formation of other martial arts.

Japan became enamored with China and Chinese culture as early as A.D. 607 when the first official Japanese embassy was sent to China. This event served to establish formal relations between the eastern islanders and the Sui dynasty rulers.[3] For several centuries thereafter a continuous flow of Chinese ideas entered the Japanese islands. The official intercourse between the two nations ceased after A.D. 894, but unofficial relations existed through the 12th century.[4] After this date a satiation point was reached and Japan isolated her frontiers, except for occasional Zen priests who journeyed between the nations. Today, Chinese influence is apparent in Japan's written language, art, architecture, religion, and in numerous subtleties of culture and etiquette, though the overt suggestion of this to many native Japanese will evoke an indignant denial. From the point of view of the student of martial arts, however, the Sinification of Japan is regarded as singularly far reaching, and thus must be studied with great care.

We cannot, on the other hand, subscribe to the theories of those who assert that the *bu-jutsu* of Japan are the direct result of Chinese influence and inspiration. Although such arts as *kempo (ch'üan fa), sumo, yawara, torite, ashikeri, ken-jutsu,* and judo could have drifted across the waterways from China at unrecorded times,[5] such a hypothesis seems untenable when viewed in the harsh light of existing facts. It may be concluded that while China was a focal point that radiated "culture" to the outside "barbarian" world, many of the aforementioned Japanese *bu-jutsu* had their beginnings in the Japanese islands exclusively.

Buddhism, the great continental philosophy, was first brought to Japan by bands of Chinese and Korean travelers[6] in the sixth century. With the founding of China's T'ang dynasty in A.D. 608, there began a period of close Chinese contacts. The resulting flow of ideas from the mainland served to firmly implant this embryonic religion in the Japanese nation, largely through the efforts of peripatetic Buddhist priests who moved back and forth freely between the two countries. Thus at the same time that its power and influence was beginning to spread to Japan, Buddhism in China was at its zenith in popularity.

In Chapter Five the theory was advanced that the Buddhist monks among various shipwrecked castaway groups had inadvertently brought a weaponless self-defense system to the Ryukyu Islands. It follows then, that, if mere accidents resulted in Okinawa's learning a Chinese weaponless martial art, the volitional residence of such Buddhist priests in Japan points rather certainly to exchanges of ideas on such techniques. Thus, there is every likelihood that the neophyte Japanese priests were taught a form of self-defense for use during their travels.

Records, travel diaries, and similar chronicles showing the routes and general histories of these early priests have never been fully analyzed—in many instances never having been seen at all by Western historians. Voluminous written materials exist in Japanese Buddhist monasteries that are generally unavailable to the laity, and even more documents exist in remote Chinese Buddhist and Taoist temples cut off completely from the world by present-day politics. Aside from the general lack of access to this valuable data, a researcher in this area must be proficient in three of the world's more esoteric and difficult languages: classical Chinese, archaic Japanese, and Indian Sanskrit. So few researchers have the requisite combination of access and language mastery that it would seem that these mysteries will remain forever unsolved. Moreover, almost all of the academicians possessing the scholarly and language capabilities necessary for study of Asian cultures have neglected the more mundane subject of military arts. This is primarily the reason why most references dealing with Asia simply refer to the assorted Oriental fighting techniques as "pugilism" or "wrestling."

A further theory exists that during the seventh and fourteenth centuries, when it was common for Japanese youths to study Buddhism in China, they learned *ch'üan fa* along with their studies and brought knowledge of this art back to their homeland.[7] Since, as we pointed out, there are such close ties between *ch'üan fa* and Buddhist philosophy, this hypothesis is far from being an extreme statement.

In the Heian period (A.D. 794–1184) Buddhist monasteries used armed bands to settle local disputes,[8] and there are enigmatic reports of priests of rival temples clashing with such violence in the streets of Heian-kyo (Kyoto), that government intervention was needed to preserve order.[9]

During the classical age of Japanese martial arts (*ca.* 1500 to 1868) the leading *bu-jutsu* men were often Buddhist monks, and they regularly displayed special knowledge and skill in unarmed forms of fighting. In fact, *ch'üan fa*, pronounced "KEM-po" in Japanese, was not known by many people outside of the Buddhist priesthood until the latter part of the 16th century.

In 1592 Hideyoshi Toyotomi, the great warlord general of Japan, effected his plan for the complete conquest of China. With the transporting of his tremendous army to Korea, the campaign which was to involve Japan in an overseas invasion for the next six years, was begun. So fierce was the combined Korean-Chinese resistance that in 1598, when Hideyoshi died, the tattered remnants of his army returned home without ever setting foot on Chinese soil. Rather, the Korean isthmus was the unfortunate site of the many clashes between the opposing military factions, and emerged from Japan's first foreign "adventure" a devastated land.

In Japanese oral tradition it is recorded that many of Hideyoshi's returning samurai brought with them a working knowledge of *ch'üan fa* (or *kempo*) and that from the 16th century onward, part of the samurai's "armament" included a punching and nerve-striking technique based on Chinese *ch'üan fa*.

The relationship of Chinese military arts to the rise of a Japanese system of weaponless self-defense is vague and not fully documented by reliable sources. We do have one accurate date, however, that is authenticated by competent historians. In 1638, during the Tokugawa period, a Chinese pottery master named Ch'en Yuan-pin (1587–1671) arrived from China to serve as a ceramics instructor for the daimyo (lord) of Owari.[10] Among his other duties, Ch'en instructed several ronin (jobless samurai) in the art of seizing a man without the use of weapons.[11] Some sources have even credited this man with the introduction of *ch'üan fa* and ju-jutsu into the Japanese islands.[12] Because of its precise date, this story is popularly circulated as the beginning of a karate-like art in Japan. Yet, knowledgeable historians will dispute this theory on the grounds that a weaponless technique called *yawara* was in existence long before Ch'en came to Japan.[13] *Yawara,* it seems, is the precursor to a form of ju-jutsu and is believed by many Japanese writers to be the earliest prototype of a native bare-handed fighting art, though in some forms of *yawara* a short rod is used. Little else is known about this art and it remains one of the most esoteric of all the existing

Japanese *bu-jutsu*. Thus, although Ch'en Yuan-pin represents a very real and documented individual, his entry into the field of weaponless arts came well after their establishment as an integral part of Japan's military arts. Jigoro Kano, the founder of modern judo, stated in 1888 that of the various arts instrumental in judo's development, ju-jutsu played the most vital role.[14] Professor Kano stated conclusively that the Chinese form of fighting without weapons (i.e., *ch'üan fa*) differs so radically from ju-jutsu that there is no chance of their interconnection, and that therefore the leverage and seizing arts are of Japanese origin.[15]

Although karate from Okinawa "officially" entered Japan with the famous Gichin Funakoshi in 1915, several Okinawan karate instructors are known to have traveled and taught in Japan as early as 1904. Full-scale public initiation to the art occurred in 1915 when Master Funakoshi demonstrated karate before a large assemblage of interested Japanese spectators at the Butoku-den in Kyoto. Thus, although karate-like styles of fighting came to Japan during the period of heavy Buddhist contacts from China, with Hideyoshi's returning armies in the 16th century, and again with Ch'en Yuan-pin in the 17th century, 1915 stands as the established date of Okinawan karate's entry into the Japanese islands.

After the impetus of 1915, karate developed rather slowly into a fully accepted Japanese *bu-jutsu*. A number of prominent karate masters (e.g., Chojun Miyagi, Choki Motobu, etc.) from the Ryukyus secured teaching assignments as instructors of karate at a few of Japan's most notable universities.

The aforementioned Chojun Miyagi lectured and taught his art at Kyoto Imperial University in 1928.[16]

In 1932 Miyagi became a "coach" in the newly formed karate department of Kansai University in Osaka, often lecturing to karate and boxing clubs located throughout the city.[17] Thus, by the time war reached the Japanese citizenry on a universal scale in 1937, karate had received a general introduction to the populace as a whole, but was much more of an integral part of both university and military life. So much so, in fact, that by the end of World War II, karate had become a special part of the secondary and college campus scene. However, the real period of karate interest, as we shall see, began in the years following World War II.

Chapter 7

Buddhism & Karate

THERE is a trend among today's karatephiles to associate karate with Buddhist philosophy. Some writers have stated categorically that the two are inseparable. We will examine the available facts in order to see whether such a hypothesis is tenable.

An inspection of the ideograph that represents the *kara* 空 portion of "karate" reveals an apparent linguistic relationship to Buddhism,[1] since the same ideograph in Buddhism represents the "void," or *sunyata. Sunyata,* the Sanskrit term for "emptiness' or "nothingness," is used to represent the ancient metaphysical concept that all basic principles of life emanate from within an infinite and pristine chaos. This capsulized definition, depending on how each of its constituent terms is defined, demonstrates the fact that *sunyata* virtually defies definition even when one's tools comprise the entire English language. With this conclusion most contemporary Buddhist philosophers agree. However, in contradistinction to their avowed dislike of such definitions, many of these same Buddhist writers and theologians have made attempts at describing and categorizing *sunyata,* such that we find an exceedingly rich and varied body of interpretations.

One of the most often cited of these interpretations

takes us deep into hoary Indian antiquity. In the second century, Nagarjuna, one of Buddhism's most-revered patriarchs, set forth *sunyata* as: "The nature of reality, or rather, of the conceptions of reality which the human mind can form."[2] Nagarjuna's idea of *sunyata* was that all things are relative and without self-nature, and that the only things that can be considered concrete or as possessing absolute properties are those that are related to other things. This is the concept of "relevance," one of the most complex of all Buddhist philosophical ideas. A complete summation of its manifold ramifications fills many volumes; and because of its esoteric nature it is generally found only in Buddhist canons.

Those scholars who link karate with *sunyata* often rely on the phase known as "nothingness," saying, in effect, that karate is a weaponless—and therefore empty-handed —art, and that it becomes a concrete "entity" only when the body is applied to the various moves and gestures that constitute the karate attack and defense repertoire. Another example of this principle is that when attacked by an aggressor, the genuine karate practitioner responds with what amounts to reflex action. Such reflex is supposedly without volition, and is therefore, as the claim goes, "relative" in the Buddhist sense of *sunyata*.

It is, of course, self-evident that the term "karate" is an abstraction having no "self-nature" or "substance," and remains so until its principles are transformed into body movements. However, care must certainly be exercised in drawing analogies from such abstrusions so that they remain within the bounds of logical derivation and do not become mere mental gymnastics. For example, it should be noted that many Buddhist concepts can be applied to any number of actions in the exterior world of the senses. And as regards karate in particular we certainly cannot discount the well-corroborated fact (see Chapter One) that the "kara" portion of "karate" as it is presently written did not come into use until about 1936, the ramifications of which we will explore in this chapter. Whether or not early *ch'üan fa* masters in China or *tode-karate* masters on Okinawa were genuinely preoccupied with Buddhist philosophy remains at the time of this writing a matter of speculation.

A recent trend among writers in the general field of Asian martial arts has been to tie in certain aspects of Buddhism with specific sporting and military techniques. The *mu* principle of Buddhism is an example of this, having been associated with both judo and kendo for a number of years. *Mu* literally means "nothing," and as such bears a cursory resemblance to the concept of *sunyata*. But after more careful philological research, one finds that *mu* more specifically refers to non-striving or non-seeking, a tie-in with Sakyamuni's doctrine of the "middle path" of no extremes rather than with *sunyata*. In judo the *mu* principle is applied when two opponents face each other before a match, the idea being to clear the mind of extraneous thoughts rather than to think about the approaching contest. If one is successful, it is claimed that his body responds perfectly from moment to moment. When observing high-ranking judoists perform, those who are aware of this concept claim that they can see it in action, and that facial expression is usually the signpost that indicates whether or not the *mu* concept is being utilized.

The *mu* principle undoubtedly comes from the older Buddhist concept of *mushin,* or "no-mind," which, incidentally, was a special form of Zen training used by the samurai of feudal Japan.[3] In essence, *mushin* is an ego-less state of the mind that frees one from fear of death or failure. Musashi Miyamoto (1582–1645), one of the great fencing masters of the Tokugawa era, expressed the idea of *mushin* in the art of *ken-jutsu* (fencing):

> *Under the sword lifted high*
> *There is hell making you tremble;*
> *But go ahead*
> *And you have the land of bliss.*[4]

A further fact from which one might conclude that karate and Buddhism are interrelated is that most countries possessing a karate-like art are either predominantly Buddhistic or have had strong Buddhist influences during their development (e.g., India, Indonesia, and Okinawa). Aside from the many coincidences of the art and the religion in the same country, there is little direct evidence to show that karate or its related fighting arts throughout Asia developed in direct association with Buddhism.

The Bodhidharma "legend" appears to be the only clear-cut exception to this statement. Bodhidharma is considered to be the founder of a school of weaponless fighting called Shaolin *ch'üan fa,* the art from which karate derived many of its techniques. This theory, however, raises a number of questions. For example, Bodhidharma's chief concern was apparently to "cultivate" the mind so that enlightenment could be achieved. It is therefore not at all unusual that he developed a system of calisthenics designed to build physical and mental vitality and to aid in the development of the power of concentration. From these special exercises called *shih pa lo han sho* evolved the Shaolin *ch'üan fa*. Because of this link with a Buddhist monk, *ch'üan fa* in general and the

Shaolin School in particular can be said to have been Buddhist inspired.

Bodhidharma's main historical significance, however, is on a different level altogether. His roles, both as the twenty-eighth patriarch after Sakyamuni (the historic Buddha) and as the first patriarch of Zen Buddhism in China, are unchallenged by most historians. Bodhidharma entered China in the sixth century, at which time Chinese civilization was already over two thousand years old. At that time the Chinese had a religious "orientation" called Taoism, which, in its content and philosophy, already bore many remarkable resemblances to the teachings that Bodhidharma came to enunciate. Though Bodhidharma is generally referred to as the "founder" of Zen in China, a Chinese monk called Hui-neng (637–713) was the real father of Chinese Zen (known as Ch'an in Mandarin after the Sanskrit *dhyana*).[5] Bodhidharma's Indian Zen seemingly could not divorce itself from the lofty metaphysics so characteristic of the bulk of Indian philosophy, and thus failed to impact upon the Chinese mind as he had hoped. On the other hand, Hui-neng introduced a Zen philosophy that was closely akin to Chinese thinking and culture. An explication of the differences involved would necessitate a volume in itself. And, though no capsulized description of Taoism or Zen could hope to explain their myriad complexities, for purposes of brevity it can be said that they are, in essence, paths to "immediate awakening" or "total spiritual insight."[6]

We have seen earlier that Bodhidharma's principal concern was with cultivating the mind so that enlightenment could be achieved. The eighteen-stroke exercise that he taught was certainly not designed for physical confrontation. Likewise, Taoism is never violent, since its ends are achieved "by noninterference *(wu-wei)*, which is a kind of psychological judo."[7] Judging from all of the foregoing evidence, one must surely question statements which assert that lethal martial arts like *ch'üan fa* and karate are inextricably interconnected with Zen and Taoism! The fact, simply stated, is that *ch'üan fa* in its inception was not a lethal art, since it was a close blood relative of Bodhidharma's Shaolin *ch'üan fa*.

And then there are those who categorize the whole Bodhidharma story as mere legend. But even if we refute the legend theory and insist on Bodhidharma's historical reality, the continued influence of Buddhism on *ch'üan fa* after his death remains highly questionable. It has until now, for example, been impossible to determine whether Ch'ueh Yuan shang-jen and Li-shao (the two *ch'üan fa* masters responsible for enlarging the *shih pa lo han sho* after the passing of Bodhidharma) had any Buddhist affiliations. It is further impossible to tell whether or not these two masters would have perpetuated any Buddhist teachings even if they had been acquainted with Bodhidharma's philosophical teachings. In fact, since Ch'ueh and Li were not contemporaries of Bodhidharma—the latter having died *ca.* A.D. 534 and the former two having lived in the Sui period (A.D. 580–618)—it is difficult to determine just how direct their confrontation actually was with Bodhidharma's Buddhism, and thus how perfectly they mastered the strict Shaolin *ch'üan fa* discipline.

Another question about the Bodhidharma "legend" stems from the fact that *ch'üan fa* is sometimes said to have flourished in China long before Bodhidharma's advent.[8] We noted in Chapter Three the tradition stating that *ch'üan fa* originated some three thousand years before the

Christian era, during the reign of the Yellow Emperor, Huang-ti.[9] If true, then it would appear that *ch'üan fa* antedates Buddhism and that there would be separate developmental patterns, even though they both originated in India.

The traditional date for the entry of Buddhism into China is the first century B.C. However, significant cultural influences were not seen until about A.D. 220, at which time Buddhism's popularity was largely restricted to the merchant and lower classes.[10] The subsequent development of Buddhism in Chinese society is complex, and while the subject is interesting it is not properly within the scope of this work. It is enough to say that at this period of development, China, which was called the "Middle Kingdom," was notably hostile to foreign influences. The Chinese considered their culture superior to those "barbarian" cultures of the outside world. From this historical fact alone we can understand why the peripatetic Buddhist monks from India were for so long treated as inferiors by the Chinese gentry.[11]

But with the persistence of ever increasing numbers of proselytizing monks, Buddhism made steady inroads into China's culture so that by the fourth century, it was solidly entrenched. During the T'ang dynasty (A.D. 618–906), Buddhism reached its pinnacle, and conversely, its ebb during the period's latter years primarily because of the increasing rivalry and strength of Taoism. Buddhism never regained the impetus it had been developing up to that time. Since the majority of the currently active *ch'üan fa* schools in China cannot be historically traced further than the Sung dynasty (1127–1279),[12] it does not seem likely that Buddhism, which lost imperial favor during the latter T'ang period, could be considered closely linked with *ch'üan fa* development. In all subsequent dynasties, Buddhism has played rather minor roles, but has never entirely dropped from sight. The most recent example came at the end of the Ch'ing period (1644–1912), when Buddhist groups openly engaged in the rebellion against the foreign Manchu dynasty. And, though the Buddhist numbers were small in comparison with the Taoist elements similarly engaged, they were outstanding in their effectiveness and were most noted for the great prowess shown by several famous monks who participated openly.

Immediately prior to the Boxer Rebellion in 1900, the leader of the Boxers, Ts'ao fu-T'ien, announced that he had received a decree from the mythical Taoist deity known as the Jade Emperor to oust the barbarians from China.[13] This is significant mainly because it showed the strength of the Taoist philosophy in Chinese political life. Taoism through the centuries had evolved, like so many other religions in the world, by a constant modification of doctrines. By 1900 the traditionally philosophical Taoism, which had so strongly influenced the development of Chinese Zen Buddhism, had gradually given way to a popular form of Taoism which featured an array of gods, demi-gods, alchemy, astrology, and other mystical practices. Ts'ao fu-T'ien's pronouncement was just such a mystical feature of contemporary "popular" Taoism. The invocation of the Jade Emperor by a leader of the Boxers indicated that Taoism had permeated the thinking of this revolutionary group, as in fact it had permeated most facets of Chinese society. Also, we saw in Chapter Three that *ch'üan fa* practice was responsible for the term "Boxers." Since Taoism was the spiritual overtone of this semi-religious Western purge, it appears that *ch'üan fa,* the art, was inextricably involved with Taoism, the religion. Thus even if one were to assume that Buddhism had played a role in the development of *ch'üan fa* philosophy, it must be concluded that it gave nearly all of its ground to Taoism by the 20th century.

Unlike the Chinese who had largely restricted the practice of Buddhism to a monastic society of monks and lay people, the Japanese readily accepted it—particularly Zen Buddhism—into all strata of their society. Zen initially came to the Japanese islands during the Kamakura period in the 12th century. During this epic era of political change in Japan many great Zen masters ruled the entire spiritual hierarchy of Japanese religious circles.[14] The samurai class in particular found Zen expression and "flavor" to their liking. It became the belief that the mastery of any of the military arts began with a foundation in Zen tenets, and that a warrior could not achieve mastery of his art without a period of dedicated Zen training. At the same time, violent death was an ever-present threat to the samurai. Practice in the meditative apsects of Zen gave them a sense of freedom from the fear of life then lived.

Zen influence in the daily lives of the Japanese populace is most markedly seen in the widely practiced art forms such as tea ceremony, flower arranging, landscaping and gardening, painting, archery, and fencing. From this list it can be seen that subtle features of Japanese life reflect Zen influence; but it is the martial arts that have retained the direct, forthright path to enlightenment that was introduced by Bodhidharma. It is this very directness that has led the many thinkers to consider martial arts as a catalyst, or "middle man," between self and universal knowledge, or enlightenment.

In Chapter Two we briefly explored the thesis that

certain forms of Asian art are related to karate, as evidenced by the unmistakable karate-like postures of scores of ancient statues and friezes in China, Japan, and India.

The *Nio Bodhisattva* of Japan, the famous guardian deity seen at the gates to many Buddhist temples, appears to be the closest facsimile of a type of *ch'üan fa,* and although the Japanese sculptures depicting fighting positions are the most common today, earlier Chinese and Indian works were the prototypes for these statues. Much of the Buddhist art in China was influenced by Graeco-Buddhist art of Northern India. During the T'ang dynasty a general classification of art found in China, Korea, and Japan was termed the "T'ang-Nara-Silla" style. Since the Buddhist statues of the Japanese pre-Nara period (A.D. 645–710) are based on Indo-Sino styles and since these works show distinct fighting positions, we have still further proof that some variety of *ch'üan fa* was practiced in ancient India and China. Although this fact may be coincidental, it also remains in consideration as an example of Buddhist influence on martial art development in China and Japan.

Since at least the seventh century, Buddhist monks in China and Japan have learned a type of *ch'üan fa,* or *kempo.* On the surface it appears that such "defensive techniques" could possess no great religious significance, particularly since their original ancestor—Bodhidharma's *shih pa lo han sho*—is said to have been designed primarily for healthful exercise. But the idea keeps arising that *ch'üan fa* or *kempo* were in actuality forms of "animated meditation," i.e., essential aids in achieving enlightenment, the goal of every serious Buddhist. Although there are no authoritative sources that can be cited in support of this assumption, this is a valid conclusion from the scraps of evidence—mostly from informants' oral testimony—

that were sifted through. It should be made clear, however, that while the moral emphasis found in contemporary karate schools is usually Buddhistic in flavor, this is but a little-understood cultural remnant of a once-magnificent fabric of Oriental culture. The quasi-Buddhist philosophy being preached by many karate schools generally approaches the point of blasphemy when it is contrasted with the physical violence and animal aggression that are subtly encouraged therein.

Karate's entry into Japan with Master Funakoshi in 1915 was much too late for it to be considered an integral part of Japan's martial arts, or for it to be considered "Zen influenced." Granted, Buddhist monks and Hideyoshi's samurai did bring into Japan a form of *ch'üan fa*. This art, however, did not reach the general masses as its practice was largely restricted to the monastic Buddhist sects and the military class.

It was not until 1936 that a council of karate masters meeting on Okinawa decided to use the "kara" ideograph in writing "karate." It is claimed that they did so because the ideograph was spiritually significant, yet this explanation loses much of its credibility when one realizes that Buddhism had never achieved significant popularity among the Okinawans. In fact, it had never been a particularly strong force in the development of spiritual thought patterns in the Ryukyus, which have been "animistic" since paleolithic times. Thus it appears that the linking of Buddhism with karate is a modern innovation, and is an attempt, perhaps, to give to a deadly fighting technique the vestiges of a moral conscience.

Chapter 8

Karate in the United States

THE FIRST seven chapters have described the formation and evolution of the fighting art called "karate." It has been established that the art is the exclusive property of Asia, Asia in its broadest sense. In fact, there is no good evidence that Western civilization has contributed to any Asian forms of unarmed combat, with the possible exception of Thai boxing where, barring the inclusion of kicking techniques, Marquis of Queensberry rules are loosely observed.

Some modern writers have been wont to observe close similarities between the Medieval European knight and the samurai warriors of Japan. This comparison, though valid on the surface, cannot be carried too far since the samurai were equally at ease fighting on the ground as from horseback, whereas their heavily armored European counterparts were often like the proverbial "fish-out-of-water" when unhorsed. What combat the steel-encased knights could participate in after the disaster of unhorsement generally involved the rather clumsy wielding of a heavy straight-sword, a battle axe, or a mace.

This and other comparisons lead to the conclusion that Western military science concerns itself largely with complex weaponry, whereas individual technique and "spirit" probably best summarize the fighting style of the East. From the time English longbows and cannon felled the flower of French knighthood at Crecy in 1346 to the present use of intercontinental missiles and intricate guidance systems, Western man has been preoccupied with the matériel of war.

If "instant genocide," then, is the West's answer to the intensely individualized martial dedication of Asia, why has the West been so completely captivated by the difficult and arduous art of karate? The answer might well be simple. The fact that the West, and particularly the United States, has in recent years been exploring with great interest the more esoteric ideas and arts of the East was the natural result of the recent Allied occupation of Japan and Korea when ancient Asian cultures came under the sharp scrutiny of thousands of military and civilian personnel. Those who found their way off of Japan's glittering Ginza discovered a "new world" in the parts of this land where the people lived in the traditional manner. Present-day "Asiaphiles" trace their interest in the Orient back to such post-World War II occupation duty, or to Korean War duty when Japan served as the staging area for the conflict across the straits.

Also to be considered is the fact that, in California at least, groundwork for the entry of these arts into the United States had been laid decades before. Chinese, Japanese, and Okinawans had been immigrating sporadically since the turn of the century, and they quite naturally brought their cultures with them. It is well known that the practice of *ch'üan fa* and karate was common within these ethnic groups.

More specifically, the late 19th century was a period of rather extensive Chinese labor migrations to the Hawaiian

Islands and the western United States. The gold fever in California and the subsequent railroad building boom were jointly responsible for the importation of thousands of indentured Chinese citizens by wealthy speculators and Chinese business groups. This labor community in California was first welcomed; but as organized labor saw the great competition offered by these contract workers from across the Pacific, a cloud of prejudice formed which soon enveloped the whole of "Chinese California." This fear of cheap Chinese labor was the cause of the so-called "Yellow Peril," an idea based on economic considerations and fanciful ideas of mass Oriental migrations and their ultimate control of the entire West Coast. This prejudice was instrumental in halting Chinese immigration to the United States and her possessions, and in the passage of a series of exclusionary laws beginning with the Chinese Exclusion Act of 1882,[1] and ending with total exclusion of Chinese laborers in 1904.[2] However, this legislation came too late to prevent the seed of Chinese culture from being planted in American soil.

Few of the immigrant Chinese adopted an Americanized way of living, since their primary interest was in fulfilling their contractual agreement with the Chinese or American hiring agent. As it turned out, however, most of the indentured workers stayed on in the United States. They constructed virtually self-contained communities called "Chinatowns"—a term first mentioned in California newspapers in 1853[3]—and lived much as they did in their native country.

It is only now becoming apparent that the intricate web of Chinese society in California was never fully understood. Chinese sojourners coming to the United States in search of the promised quick wealth brought with them all the prejudices, fears, and rivalries that had existed in their homeland. A series of district companies based on ties with China-based companies, along with fraternal associations based on surname or place of origin in China, governed the Chinese sojourners' lives so completely that in many instances they were little more than slaves. Merchant companies, called *kongsi,* were formed and headed by members of the Chinese merchant class.[4] At the same time secret societies *(hui)* existed which controlled massive groups of Chinese laborers by the threat of death. Behind a façade of benevolence these organizations, in the 1850's and later, oppressed their countrymen to the point where incidents of violence became common between various Chinese groups.[5] Coupled with the fact that rival factions fought bitterly for supremacy in certain spheres of commerce (e.g., gambling and prostitution rights to labor camps) it is small wonder that Chinatowns in the West saw blood purges on a regular basis. In one of the most notable feuds, the *Hung Shun-T'ang,* which controlled San Francisco's Chinatown, clashed with the *I-Hing T'ang,* a group controlling the mining districts' Chinese laborers. Traditional feuds were also carried on, such as those between *Hakka* and *Punti* Chinese, and the more frequent battles between *kongsi* factions representing their counterparts in Canton and Hong Kong.[6] Blacksmiths in Trinity County, California, were hired to make the traditional Chinese weapons of war such as tridents, spears, pike poles, brush scythes, and bamboo shields.[7] Some rival companies even held public drills and parades in the mining town streets.[8] Amused non-Chinese workers lined the perimeter of the battle to cheer and to bet on their favorites, and some went as far as to serve as mercenaries with one or more of the rival factions.

Americans in the western United States, and particularly California, came to know of these battles as "tong wars," because in the United States the Chinese secret societies were called "tongs," which is the Cantonese pronunciation of the ideograph 堂 *t'ang,* meaning "hall" or "office."[9] The most notorious *t'ang* "enforcers" were called "hatchet men" *(boo tow doy)* because of the meat cleaver that they so skillfully wielded when dispatching opponents. Most of these "hatchet men" were also skilled in the *ch'üan fa* fighting techniques and other intricate arts such as pin-blowing and coin-flipping. Pin-blowing is an art common to several Asian countries, but most notably China and Japan. The technique is simple. An expert carries a number of sharpened pins in his mouth and blows one out at a time with a quick exhaling action. Superspies *(ninja)* in feudal Japan are said to have perfected pin-blowing to an amazing degree of accuracy up to a twenty-foot distance.

Coin-flipping consists of throwing, or flipping with the thumb, a coin whose edges have been honed to razor-sharpness. The primary targets are the jugular vein and the eye. Proponents of this art can stand, arms folded, and with a simple motion imbed a heavy coin half its width into a hardwood backstop. (This fact can be attested to, the author having seen such a demonstration in Honolulu in 1961.)

In 1898 San Francisco police Lieutenant William Price estimated that of the less than three thousand "highbinders" (the term given these "hatchet men" in California) in San Francisco, between three hundred and five hundred earned some part of their living by killing for hire.[10]

An interesting feature of the many California *t'angs* was

their close affiliation with the Triad Lodges in China and Southeast Asia.[11] The Chinese Triad Society was a 17th-century organization formed for the specific purpose of subverting the controlling power in China at that time, the Manchu dynasty. When this group was broken up by Manchu forces in the 18th century, five Buddhist monks secretly reorganized the Five Provincial Grand Lodges of the Triad Society, and continued working secretly to overthrow the Manchus.[12] Tradition states that these five monks were *ch'üan fa* masters and that for many years they instructed masses of people in the use of the art as an offensive tactic against the Manchu soldiers.

A police raid on a secret society in San Francisco in 1853 showed that the group was an American arm of a Chinese-based Triad faction. At that time the combined Triad forces controlled the walled city of Shanghai by force of arms, and were largely dependent on financial assistance from their brethren on this side of the Pacific.[13] The American Triad Societies exacted heavy conscriptions from their members—whether willing or not—in sums as high as $150,000 a year,[14] and made further profits by conducting illicit businesses such as gambling, prostitution, and trafficking in opium.[15]

As the Chinese in the western United States became increasingly better accepted by American society, their role as menial laborers underwent a marked change. They worked predominantly as farmers, merchants, laundrymen, and cafe proprietors, and many chose to sever their ties with China and take American citizenship. This, combined with the crackdown on vice in Chinatowns throughout California, helped put an end to the *t'ang*'s iron grip on the American-Chinese community, so that by 1930 the Triad Society was a thing of the past.

Ch'üan fa, used offensively at the height of the *t'ang* crisis, once again became an exercise ritual and holiday spectacle for the Chinese community. Most American-Chinese societies sponsored *ch'üan fa* practices, limiting participation to those of immediate Chinese ancestry. The slow opening of *ch'üan fa* to non-Chinese practitioners did not come until two decades after World War II.

With *t'ang* warfare and intense racial discrimination headlining the troubled activities of the Chinese in California, many Chinese emigrants chose to disembark in the then Kingdom of Hawaii. They generally fared much better in their relations with each other and with their non-Chinese bosses. Organizations similar to the *t'ang* and *hui* groups of western America were founded in Hawaii, and by 1889 the first Chinese society—the Ket On Association—was born.[16] As the Chinese had no consular representatives in the Hawaiian Islands (then a monarchy ruled by Queen Liliuokalani), it became the Ket On Association's function to aid members of the Chinese community in legal matters and in "benevolent practices" (e.g., obtaining burial funds for indigent Chinese, etc.).[17] Most of the Chinese societies which formed after the Ket On Association were exclusive, in that they limited membership to those whose ancestry could be traced to a specific Chinese district or province.[18]

It has been previously noted that overseas Chinese communities have typically been isolated, introverted, and highly exclusive as regards their ethnic arts and crafts. Since earliest recorded history, the Chinese have maintained extreme pride in their indigenous arts and have guarded their public exhibition and knowledge very closely. Thus it is understandable that these societies continued to be restrictive on the basis of surname or location of ancestry in China, and that an art like *ch'üan fa,* which was very restrictive in China, would remain so in Hawaii. To some extent, *ch'üan fa* was practiced within the confines of these societies as a calisthenics type of physical exercise. These exercise sessions, though not officially sponsored by the various societies, were generally conducted by members who had achieved recognition for their *ch'üan fa* skills in the Chinese province from which they came.

In 1922 the Chinese Physical Culture Association was founded in Honolulu, Hawaii, to promote physical culture among the islands' Chinese communities.[19] This club was the first organization to practice *ch'üan fa* (known in Hawaii by the popular term "kung-fu") in organized classes with several instructors from different Chinese provinces.[20] This association remains alive and very active today.

Non-Chinese were able to gain fleeting glimpses of *ch'üan fa* techniques both in Hawaii and most of California during the Chinese New Year celebration held in February. This is the most lavishly celebrated of the Chinese holy days, and there are records of the famous dragon dances and fireworks displays taking place in California as early as the 1850's.[21] The dragon and lion dances are highlights of the New Year, and are the major source of attraction for tourists visiting the various Chinatowns. Almost unnoticed, and very rarely understood when observed, are the accompanying *ch'üan fa* acrobatics generally performed by the young Chinese representatives of the *ch'üan fa* clubs. Though never lacking in enthusiasm, these boys are rarely adept at the art of *ch'üan fa* and thus attract less attention to the art than would highly skillful exponents.

This, it seems, is done purposely by the heads of the organizational hierarchy of the Chinese societies. However, according to a spokesman of the United Chinese Society—the "parent" organization for all Chinese societies in the Hawaiian Islands—*ch'üan fa* has not purposely been kept from the non-Chinese, nor are there any written rules that specifically exclude non-Chinese from participating in *ch'üan fa* associations.[22] But it is evident that, notwithstanding the absence of a clearly documented policy, there has long been an unwritten law prohibiting non-Chinese from participation in the numerous Chinese societies' activities. (The author in fact attempted to secure *ch'üan fa* instruction in 1958 at the Chinese Physical Culture Association in Honolulu, and was refused admission. Although other reasons were given, it was evident that the real reason for rejection was non-Chinese ancestry.) It can be concluded that in practice, *ch'üan fa* had been restrictive on the basis of national origin in the Hawaiian Islands as well as elsewhere until 1957.

Mr. Tinn Chan Lee, an expert in the *T'ai Chi Ch'üan* form of *ch'üan fa,* is the first Chinese martial arts instructor known to have opened his teachings to the general public. Mr. Lee began *T'ai Chi* classes at the Mun Lum School (Chinese language school) in Honolulu in 1957.[23] Since that initial public class, Mr. Lee has instructed various clubs and organizations, and given lecture-demonstrations to numbers of Asian study groups.

Since Mr. Lee is a naturalized citizen from China, his background is quite interesting. He first came to Hawaii in 1923 where he worked in the electronics field. In 1937 he returned to China to renew his *ch'üan fa* training that had begun when he was very young. His instructor was one of the two great living proponents of *T'ai Chi*

Ch'üan, Master Kam Chin Wu. After receiving an advanced degree, he returned to Honolulu and soon opened an electrical repair and appliance store which he operates to the present day.

When dealing with a person with as interesting a personal history as Mr. Lee's, one is very likely to wonder why a naturalized Chinese-American instead of a second or third generation Chinese-American would be the first to break the traditional barrier of *ch'üan fa* secrecy. The first of two possible explanations is that the art of *T'ai Chi Ch'üan* is one of the less apparently "lethal" forms of *ch'üan fa,* though in the hands of experts *T'ai Chi* is certainly an effective fighting art. It is popularly practiced by Chinese of all ages for its health-giving benefits, as was seen in the recently filmed documentary of life in contemporary China entitled "Beyond the Great Wall." In certain parts of the film elderly men could be seen performing the graceful movements of this style of *ch'üan fa.* In fact, Mr. Lee's stated premise for including non-Chinese in his *T'ai Chi* classes was based on the physical culture aspect of such teaching.[25] The second reason may be that Lee felt a patriotic duty toward the United States, and wanted to express his thanks for the hospitality he had received and for the benefits of being a citizen of his adopted country [26] This type of loyalty, as we shall see later in the chapter, has not been uncommon among naturalized Americans of Asian ancestry.

Modern Hawaii has been called the "melting pot" of the world due to the large-scale intermarriage of members of its ethnic communities. In breaking the population into ethnic groups we see that the Japanese constitute at least one-third of the islands' total population (which traditionally includes those of Okinawan ancestry). The

Chinese make up the next largest Oriental segment, followed by members of the American-Korean community.[27]

The great bulk of Okinawan emigrants came to Hawaii between 1880–1910.[28] As Okinawa was then politically a part of the Japanese Empire, these people were classified as Japanese in the various census polls. In 1924 the Japanese Consulate General for Hawaii listed the Okinawan population as 16,536 or 13.8 per cent of the total Japanese population.[29] If there has been no great difference in rate of population growth between Okinawans and non-Okinawan-Japanese since that time, we can estimate that in 1950 there were about 26,000 people of direct Okinawan ancestry living on all of the islands of Hawaii.

Following the United States' 19th-century policy of excluding further Chinese labor immigrations, the Hawaiian legislature in 1887 and 1888 enacted similar laws to stop the flow of Chinese field workers.[30] As the American planters living in the Hawaiian Islands then needed a substitute for the loss of their invaluable Chinese plantation hands, they turned to Japan as their next source of cheap labor. Although a small scattering of Japanese emigrants had come to Hawaii as early as 1868,[31] their greatest numbers arrived between 1885 and 1894—nearly 30,000 in all.[32] By 1900 Hawaii had over 61,000 Japanese, or about 40 per cent of the total population.[33]

The Hawaiian government, alarmed by the explosion of the Japanese population, finally refused further admission of Japanese contract workers, and returned to Japan over a thousand recently arrived laborers.[34] Japanese diplomats regarded this non-admission policy as an insult, and sent a warship along with a demand for indemnification.

Upon tacit approval of the United States, which was then in the process of annexing these islands, Hawaii did pay an indemnity of $75,000, after which Japan withdrew her complaint.[35]

Shortly thereafter, Japanese immigration to U.S. possessions was hindered by the so-called "Gentlemen's Agreement" which stopped the labor migrations in exchange for an American commitment promising no open discrimination against the Japanese already in the country.[36] Two decades later, Congress passed the "Japanese Exclusion Act,"[37] which arose out of anti-Japanese feelings that had been developing in California. This antagonism had evolved from a rather vaguely stated concept that the Japanese constituted a threat to the security of California because of their general adherence to the cultural patterns of their homeland. It has been argued, however, that the primary fear was of the agricultural prowess of the Japanese family farms, which were producing more cash crops per acre than their Caucasian counterparts. Had it not been for President Theodore Roosevelt's firm stand for fairer treatment of the Japanese on the West Coast, these people would undoubtedly have experienced even more intensely prejudicial treatment than they did.[38] After 1924, immigration from Japan and Okinawa virtually ceased, except for small numbers of teachers, students, "picture brides," priests, *kibei* (those born in the United States, but sent to Japan for their education), and persons with temporary visas.

As Chinese *ch'üan fa* had come with the earliest Chinese sojourners to mainland United States and the Hawaiian Islands, so did karate enter with Okinawan immigrants. Most Okinawans who emigrated to Hawaii and California prior to 1903 generally lacked training in this art due to its secrecy and selectivity. However, an Okinawan immigrant in Honolulu who had begun his karate training at the age of nine in 1894 in Naha, Okinawa, had continued for eleven years before coming to Hawaii in 1905.[39] From 1903 onward those with an educational background knew at least the fundamental basics of karate, since, beginning in 1903, karate became a standard part of the Okinawan schools' physical education program. In fact, every boy who reached the intermediate grades received karate instruction. The number of karate practitioners among Okinawan immigrants in Hawaii and California is virtually impossible to gauge.

Undoubtedly many Okinawans have been practicing the art throughout most of their lives. Few, however, advertised knowledge of their karate skills or undertook to teach others their art. The reason for this seems to have been the traditional secrecy which karate underwent after Satsuma's invasion of the Ryukyus in 1609, and the fact that during the early days after Japan's formal annexation of these islands in 1875 the various karate schools of Naha, Shuri, and Tomari engaged each other in competitions that amounted to combat. Okinawan emigrants from these villages carried the old hostilities with them to their new homes in the West. Very few wanted to openly teach karate for fear that a rival would learn their secrets. Thus, karate remained more of a family art than something that was available to all of the Okinawan community.

It is also true that most of the Okinawan sojourners lacked sufficient training in karate to instruct others in the art. A majority of the karate students simply practiced the various *kata* movements in the privacy of their homes. It was not until 1927 that the first recognized master of karate entered the Hawaiian Islands.

Kensu Yabu, one of the early Okinawan karate masters and a retired lieutenant of the Japanese Army, introduced his form of the art to Hawaii in 1927. While returning from a personal business trip to the mainland United States, Yabu was persuaded by a group of Okinawan citizens to stop in the islands for a short while for the purpose of teaching karate. Yabu consented to do so, and taught karate in the private homes of a number of Okinawans.[40] In April, 1927, he presented the first public karate demonstration at the Nuuanu YMCA in Honolulu, and although the demonstration was open to the public nearly all of the spectators were Okinawans.[41]

Kensu Yabu traveled to the island of Kauai, Territory of Hawaii, in the latter part of April giving lectures and karate demonstrations at a number of towns.[42] After approximately five months of teaching karate in the Hawaiian Islands, Master Yabu returned to his home on Okinawa.

The ramifications of Yabu's short visit to Hawaii were manifold. First, non-Okinawans witnessed for the initial time a karate performance by a recognized authority. The few *naichi* Japanese (i.e., Japanese from one of the four main islands of Japan) who observed Yabu's YMCA demonstration saw karate to be a strong fighting art, possibly even stronger than their judo. This interest in karate by non-Okinawans thereafter ebbed and flowed until the post-World War II period. Yabu's arrival did the effect of solidifying the Okinawan karate enthusiasts in Hawaii who had previously studied only in the seclusion of their homes. His open teachings brought interested groups of Okinawans together for practice and recreation, something the rivalries of Naha, Shuri, and Tomari had prevented on Okinawa.

The Hawaii of the late 1920's and early 1930's saw promoters matching judoists against boxers. Since such contests were publicly acclaimed and highly profitable, a group of Okinawan men decided to combine their resources and bring from Okinawa a karate expert to pit against some of the well-known island fighters.[43] This promotional group selected the famous Choki Motobu as their karate champion.

Motobu's history reads much like a Hemingway characterization. He was reputed to have defeated Russia's heavyweight boxing champion in a bare-handed contest in 1924.[44] Although documentation for this bout is lacking, Motobu's reputation as a strongman and fighter is legendary among contemporary Okinawan and Japanese peoples. Complications arose, however, over Motobu's visa and he was not permitted to remain in Hawaii after arriving at the Immigration Station in 1932.[45] The United States Immigration Office does not release classified information concerning immigrants, and so their refusal to grant Motobu a temporary visa will never be completely understood. On the other hand, speculation centers around Motobu's record as a brawler, which, in their opinion served to brand him as an undesirable.

Undaunted by this initial failure in promoting karate versus boxing the aforementioned Okinawan group attempted to bring to Hawaii other karate experts for this purpose. Their second selection was two Okinawan students of high moral caliber, both of whom had studied at leading Japanese universities. They were Zuiho Mutsu and Kamesuke Higaonna.

Mutsu and Higaonna came to Hawaii in 1933 with the understanding that they would be teaching and lecturing on the art of karate, not exhibiting their art in the boxing ring.[46] Both flatly refused to engage in the proposed matches on the grounds that karate was too dangerous for such contests.[47]

Thomas Miyashiro, son of an Okinawan immigrant, had studied with Yabu in 1927, and was thus a highly respected member of the Okinawan community in Hawaii. He convinced most of the Okinawan karate enthusiasts to approach Mutsu and Higaonna en masse and request that they remain in Hawaii to teach karate publicly.[48] The two Okinawan *sensei* agreed, and soon thereafter opened a school at the Asahi Photo Studio near Honolulu's Aala Park.[49] Miyashiro joined the teaching staff as assistant instructor and interpreter, and soon the school was filled with Okinawan-American and Japanese-American students. Because of the rapidity with which the school grew, larger quarters were soon needed. The new site chosen was the Izumo Taisha Shinto Mission near the intersection of King and Beretania Streets, also in Honolulu.

A club was formed from these classes, called the Hawaii Karate Seinin Kai (Hawaii Young People's Karate Club).[50] Shortly thereafter this group staged a public demonstration at the Honolulu Civic Auditorium.[51] A number of Caucasian spectators viewing this display became interested in learning karate. Most of these young men were members of the First Methodist Church located on Beretania Street, next to the Honolulu Academy of Arts. Through their efforts, in 1933 there was formed the first known Caucasian group in the Western world to openly study and sponsor karate activities.[52]

The three instructors of the Hawaii Karate Seinin Kai presided over each karate practice held several nights a week in the church basement. The most remarkable thing about this development is the fact that at that period of history there did not exist the rapport that is presently enjoyed between Asian and non-Asian peoples. In fact, these young Caucasians and all others who studied Oriental arts in the pre-World War II period were considered eccentric and were highly criticized by certain segments of the Caucasian community.

A Lieutenant Moore of the Army Air Corps, coach of the Wheeler Air Field's boxing and wrestling teams, was a member of this church group's karate class. His efforts and interest in karate, coupled with help from Mr. Miyashiro, brought visiting Okinawan karate instructors and students to Wheeler Air Field for karate instruction.[53] It is very likely that the American military's first contact with karate occurred at this time, a scant eighteen years after the art's formal introduction into Japan by Gichin Funakoshi.

Late in 1933 Mutsu returned to Japan to resume his duties as vice-president of Imperial University's (presently Tokyo University) Karate Study Club.[54] Higaonna returned to Japan shortly thereafter at which time Mr. Miyashiro assumed leadership of the Hawaii Karate Seinin Kai. He elected to continue classes at the Izumo Taisha Mission, First Methodist Church, and Wheeler Field, and to open several new locations in rural Oahu.

Until now karate had remained a very esoteric art. Though most Japanese- and Okinawan-American participants understood that there was a fundamental philosophy underlying karate practice, few others were aware that there was any more to it than the physical defense techniques.

Due primarily to the Okinawan community's interest in furthering karate practice in Hawaii, Mr. Chinei Kinjo, editor of the Okinawan newspaper *Yoen Jiho Sha* published on the island of Kauai, invited the famous Okinawan karate master Chojun Miyagi to come to Hawaii in 1934 to teach karate.[55] Co-sponsors of Miyagi's trip were the Lihue Young Buddhist Association's Judo Club and the Okinawa Ken-Jin Kai (Okinawa Prefectural People's Club).[56]

For the Hawaiian Islands to receive such a renowned master of karate was indeed a fortunate occurrence. His impact on the local scene can best be gleaned from a translation of the *Yoen Jiho Sha's* article of May 1, 1934:

Long awaited Mr. Miyagi finally arrives. . . .

Chojun Miyagi, the recognized authority of Ryukyu karate and master of unmeasurable skill, was prepared to visit Hawaii on invitation of this company. But due to various difficulties his departure from Okinawa has been postponed many times. Anxious karate fans of the Hawaiian Islands, who were looking forward to seeing him, began sending inquiries as to the exact date of his arrival. . . . We are relieved to hear from Mr. Miyagi by telegram, on the 26th, "Am leaving today."

Many requests have been received from various islands to the effect that in the event of his arrival he ought to visit that island first, but upon his arrival, after one or two demonstrations in Honolulu first, we will ask him to go completely around this island (Kauai). We are considering asking him to visit other islands afterward.

Soon after the announcement of the forthcoming visit of Mr. Chojun Miyagi, we were approached by Policemen . . . of Waimea expressing the desire of the police department to give demonstrations for the policemen of this island. Since we acknowledge their request gladly, we will consult Mr. Miyagi when he arrives and it seems that the exhibition will take place in the presence of all the policemen of this island.

Concerning the visit, well wishers of the various islands had tremendous expectation and many pledged their support. . . .

As already reported, Mr. Miyagi is the master of karate at Taiiku Kyokai (Health Institute) operated by the Government of Okinawa and as far as his profound knowledge in his art is concerned, no one in all of Okinawa prefecture can equal him. In Okinawa he participates where ever karate is practiced. Prior to his departure to Hawaii, he conducted a one-week seminar . . . sponsored by the Okinawa Branch of the Dai Nippon Butoku-kai. Studying until October 1915 under the supervision of the late Kanjuu Toonda, reknowned master of Chinese kempo (ch'üan fa), he sought profound knowledge. Twice he went to . . . China, once in May of 1915 and . . . in July of 1917, and studied and made research on the Chinese art. . . . In 1926 he planned to improve and unify karate. In order to carry out his plan he rallied his companions and established the Okinawa Karate-Jutsu Kenkyu Kai (Okinawa Karate Research Club). . . . In 1926, he accepted a part-time professorship at the First Budo Seminar under the auspices of the Dai Nippon Butoku-kai Okinawa Committee. He was invited to be karate instructor in the Judo Department of Kyoto University in October 1928. . . . In June 1932, he was invited by the Karate Department of Kansai University in Osaka, where he coached karate. In May 1932, he visited

Tokyo. By earnest request of karate and boxing clubs of various schools in the city, he conducted lectures and gave demonstrations. . . .[57]

Miyagi's arrival in Hawaii created quite a stir among the islands' martial arts devotees. He toured a number of towns in rural Oahu and Honolulu to answer their requests for karate demonstrations. The popularity of the Okinawan master was such that great numbers of Caucasians came to observe his karate lecture-demonstrations, and they moved one newspaper reporter to remark "this is true karate."[58] In the latter part of May, 1934, Miyagi traveled to the island of Kauai where he performed in Waimea, Hanalei, Koloa, and Hanapepe, and gave a series of special demonstrations to the island's police force.

On May 29, 1934, an article in the *Yoen Jiho Sha* advertised that students wishing to learn *kempo-karate* should apply immediately for such instruction. The term "kempo-karate" should be remembered because future instructors in these arts used this combination in the post-World War II period. "Kempo" is simply the Japanese way of pronouncing the Chinese ideographs representing the word "ch'üan fa." Miyagi continued his teaching on Kauai until January 15, 1935, at which time he returned to Okinawa where business matters demanded his personal attention.[59] His sojourn in Hawaii lasted approximately eight months, during which time he directly assisted over a hundred karate students.

Except for Thomas Miyashiro's karate classes in Professor Henry Okazaki's judo gymnasium which continued to 1936,[60] Miyagi's return to Okinawa in 1935 virtually ended the short but dynamic period of karate establishment and growth in Hawaii. From then to 1942 a period of quiet prevailed in Hawaiian karate circles. The Hawaii Karate Seinin Kai ceased to exist after Mr. Miyashiro's retirement and for several years following 1936 there were no known karate instructors openly teaching the art. As in the pre-1927 era, karate practice returned to the Okinawan community where small groups continued in semi-private. The great interest in karate fostered by Yabu, Mutsu, Higaonna, Miyagi, and Miyashiro, would not be rekindled until a Hawaiian born Japanese-American named James M. Mitose entered the martial arts scene at the outbreak of the Second World War.

Virtually all of the Hawaiian-born karate enthusiasts felt that karate was a post-World War II phenomenon. This misassumption is based both on the lack of knowledge of the 1927–1936 era and the fact that Dr. Mitose's style was not karate at all, but was the remote ancestor, *Shorinji Kempo* (Japanese way of pronouncing *Shaolin ch'üan fa*). It was not until after the Korean conflict that karate per se made its reappearance.

Dr. Mitose was born in Hawaii in 1916. At age five he was sent to Kyushu, Japan, for schooling in his ancestor's art of self-defense called Kosho-ryu Kempo. From 1921 to 1936 he studied and mastered this art which is based directly on Bodhidharma's *Shaolin ch'üan fa*.[61] The Mitose family tradition states that members of their clan in Kumamoto and Nagasaki brought the knowledge of *Shaolin ch'üan fa* from China shortly before the Tokugawa era, which began in 1600. This art was modified through the years by successive Mitose *kempo* masters until the *Kosho-ryu,* or "Old Pine Tree Style," *kempo* was born.[62] Mitose's *kempo* is not Okinawan karate, a fact made abundantly clear by Mitose's explanation of the many facets

15. Rev. Dr. James M. Mitose *(left)* and author Haines discuss the former's background as a *kempo* master of the Kosho-ryu School. *Photograph by Richard White.*

of *kempo* that do not involve combative techniques. However, some of the *kata* forms of the *Kosho-ryu* resemble, and in a few instances are duplicated in, certain styles of karate. This is certainly to be expected when one realizes how heavily Okinawan karate borrowed from Chinese *ch'üan fa*. An example of similarity between *Kosho-ryu Kempo* and Okinawan karate is found in the *kata* called *nai-han-chi*. Dr. Mitose explains that the philosophical significance of this *kata,* seldom if ever acknowledged in karate, is always explained to a student of *Kosho-ryu Kempo* before the physical combat forms are taught.[63]

Kosho-ryu Kempo is truly a remarkable art. In essence, the ideals of Zen Buddhism as expounded by Bodhidharma and the great Zen master and patriarch Rinzai (Lin-chih), are fundamental to the physical manifestations of the *Kosho-ryu* fighting art. The development of restraint, propriety, humbleness, and integrity, therefore, are the cornerstones of *Kosho-ryu Kempo,* and the actual combat techniques merely one of the many modes of reaching these goals. *Kempo* training in its entirety consists of intensive instruction in Buddhist philosophy, general education, and the human body and its systems, as well as training in kendo (fencing), *kyu-do* (archery), *ikebana* (flower arranging), swimming, tree-climbing, horsemanship, use of the blowgun, and the weaponless forms of traditional *Shaolin ch'üan fa.*[64]

Kosho-ryu Kempo, therefore, is more than just another style of unarmed self-defense; it is a way of life complete with a socially significant philosophy that is capsulized in the term "Self-Defense." Only in the most extreme instances of life-threatening aggression are the fighting arts brought into play; and even then they are designed to bring the opponent to the awareness of his wrong rather than to maim or injure him.

After completing his training in Japan, Dr. Mitose returned to Hawaii in 1936.[65] The final incidents leading up to World War II, contrasted with America's previously quasi-cordial involvement with the Japanese Empire, placed Dr. Mitose in the complex role of dual loyalties, as was the case of all *kibei.* Mitose explains his feelings at that time:

For my position was different from that of most Americans. I had lived happily in America as an American citizen. I loved America and its institutions and felt it was my duty to take up arms for this country whose privileges had been generously extended to me. On the other hand it was not as simple a decision as it would be for most. I had spent the formative years of my life in Japan, and had some relatives still living in Japan to whom I was bound by every tie of blood and experiences shared in common.[66]

On December 8, 1941, less than twenty-four hours after Japan's successful strike against the United States Naval Base at Pearl Harbor, James Mitose made his decision and entered the Hawaii Territorial Guard.[67] Feeling that his *kempo* art should then be shared with the country of his birth, Territory of Hawaii, U.S.A., Dr. Mitose, in 1942, organized the Official Self-Defense Club at the Beretania Mission in Honolulu for the purpose of teaching ". . . the true meaning of self-defense."[68] This organization lasted until 1953 under the leadership of Mitose,[69] and is now in the hands of one of his disciples, Thomas Young.

Because of Dr. Mitose's intense dedication to the *kempo* "way of life," he was somewhat of an enigma to the sportsminded people of Hawaii, as well as to many who studied with him. When the doors of the Official Self-Defense Club opened for the first time, the majority of aspirants to respond were non-Okinawan, non-Japanese. It seemed inevitable that these people would be unable to fully comprehend—much less to live up to—the total life-involvement required by the study of *Kosho-ryu Kempo,* and that most of them would not want Oriental morality mixed in with their martial arts training. The fundamental disparity that then arose between master and pupils naturally limited the number of students that would choose to pursue *kempo* studies. Thus, at the time of Mitose's departure for the United States mainland in 1953, only five pupils—Thomas Young, William Chow, Paul

Yamaguchi, Arthur Keawe, and Edward Lowe—had attained the *shodan* or black-belt degree.[70]

After ten years of attempting to teach the gamut of skills that comprised *Kosho-ryu Kempo,* Dr. Mitose wrote a book entitled *What Is Self-Defense?.* In it he explained his position and philosophy in regard to self-defense study; but at the insistence of the publisher, the book included hundreds of photos of self-defense techniques. Thus the average reader is led to believe that, indeed, this is merely another empty-handed martial art. Shortly thereafter, Dr. Mitose retired from active *kempo* instruction and left the Hawaiian Islands for the United States, there to pursue the studies that ultimately led to his ordination as a Christian minister, and the attainment of the doctors of theology and philosophy degrees.

Kempo arts did not expire after Dr. Mitose left the Hawaiian Islands; rather, an increased interest in unarmed combat grew due to the teachings of the Mitose graduates. Three of his *shodan* grantees formed clubs of their own, while the fourth, Thomas Young, assumed control of the Official Self-Defense Club.

Thomas Young, a soft-spoken and intelligent American-Chinese, probably best epitomized the type of individual Mitose was looking for when he began *kempo* instruction in 1942. Young was a student of *ch'üan fa* in his youth and his interest in these arts led him to seek out Mitose when he learned of *Kosho-ryu Kempo.* He began his training in this art primarily because of deep involvement with the principles of self-defense as expounded in Dr. Mitose's *Kosho-ryu Kempo* philosophy.[71] As of 1966, Mr. Young had graduated a number of *shodan,* including some who have gone on to form *kempo* clubs in Hawaii and on the mainland United States.[72]

Two other former Mitose pupils stand out on today's Hawaiian martial arts scene. They are William Chow and Edward "Bobby" Lowe. Chow received his *shodan* in 1946, and three years later formed his own club at the Nuuanu YMCA.[73] The unusual aspect of this organization was the fact that it was called a "kempo-karate" school. As Mitose has never associated *Kosho-ryu Kempo* with Okinawan karate in any manner, it is difficult to understand this move by Chow. *"Kempo-karate,"* was first used in 1934 when the *Yoen Jiho Sha* newspaper advertised for prospective students for Chojun Miyagi's Hawaiian visit. And, since Miyagi was well aware that *kempo* and *ch'üan fa* were synonymous, his choice of the term probably meant that his style of karate *(Goju-ryu)* was a combination of Chinese *ch'üan fa* and Okinawan karate. Perhaps Chow's use of the word "karate," which was far better known in Hawaii than "kempo," was simply his way of attracting more students to his school. But however that may be, William Chow has trained and awarded the *shodan* to a large number of students since 1949, all of whom claim mastery in this nebulous art of "kempo-karate." Edward Lowe's significance will be discussed in conjunction with the post-Korean War karate development.

*   *   *   *

The re-entry of "pure" or Okinawan karate to the active Hawaiian martial arts picture occurred in 1956, though the roots had taken hold after World War II when many servicemen were stationed in Japan. Many Hawaiian-born second *(nisei)* and third *(sansei)* generation Japanese-Americans found occupation duty in their ancestral homeland an enlightening experience. Most of them, having been reared in contact with grandparents whose memories of Japan were still fresh, had a "feeling" for these arts which by then had been identified with Japanese culture, and so many took up the study of karate, some even studying with the great names of Japanese karate. These *nisei* and *sansei* were shortly to become the "new breed," as it were, of American karate.

Such, for example, was Carlton Shimomi. By organizing the *Shorin-ryu* karate club on Kapahulu (Honolulu), in August of 1956, he became the first to reintroduce "pure" karate into the Hawaiian Islands.[74] Shimomi had studied *Shorin-ryu* karate in Fukuoka, Japan, while a member of the armed forces. This style, founded in the Ryukyu Islands, was brought to Japan after 1915 and grew in popularity until it became one of the styles that is practiced in Japanese universities today.

Walter Nishioka, another *Shorin-ryu* expert, followed quickly in Carlton Shimomi's footsteps by organizing the Goshinkai Karate School in July of 1957. Nishioka received his *shodan* in Japan, and had studied for a length of time on Okinawa as well.[75]

Chojun Miyagi's *Goju-ryu* karate was reactivated in the Hawaiian Islands by Mitsugi Kobayashi, George Miyasaki, and Kenneth Murakami. The latter two, while in the Air Force, studied in Kawasaki City, Japan, with one of the few existing *ju-dan* (10th degree) in karate today, Professor Kanki Izumikawa. Upon returning to Hawaii they established the Senbukan, Hawaii Branch, Goju-ryu Karate School. Kobayashi received his training from the famous master Higa of Okinawa while working for the United States Civil Service,[76] and opened the Kobayashi Dojo in Hawaii after completing his service on Okinawa.

Since Okinawan karate's reintroduction into Hawaii by Carlton Shimomi in 1956, there has been a steady

16. George Miyasaki, Goju-ryu pioneer in Hawaii, instructs advanced student in *sanchin* breathing exercise.

increase in the number of competing schools, or styles *(ryu)*. Although many of these styles are orthodox karate forms, it has become an all-too-common practice for an individual to earn the *shodan* in two or more *ryu* and then to teach what he feels are the best techniques of each. The results are quite evident. For example, of the five Mitose graduates only Thomas Young stayed with the *kempo* style of his teacher. "Bobby" Lowe probably deviated from *Kosho-ryu Kempo* the most markedly, since in 1958 he affiliated his school of self-defense with Masatatsu Oyama's Kyokushinkai of Tokyo. Oyama's style is known for its lethality and for the violence which it has been wont to display. In fact, Oyama gained notoriety by touring various areas of the world and killing a number of full-grown bulls with his bare hands under controlled conditions. His compact with Mr. Lowe is stated in the following letter:

The Hawaii Kyokushinkai is affiliated with the Tokyo Kyokushinkai and was designated on 15 November, 1958 as the bona-fide representative in Honolulu of the Nippon Karate-do Kyokushinkai and is fully qualified to use . . . styles of Oyama dojo.[77]

This type of affiliation is still being carried on today. Other graduates of the "Mitose line" have continually traveled to Japan for further training and it seems likely that little of the original *Kosho-ryu Kempo* will survive another decade of karate growth.

In June, 1959 five men formed the Hawaii Karate Association. They were Paul Yamaguchi, a Mitose graduate; Carlton Shimomi of *Shorin-ryu Karate;* and instructors Mitsugi Kobayashi, George Miyasaki, and Kenneth Murakami of *Goju-ryu Karate.*[78]

By 1961 these same instructors, plus a number of newer faces, combined to form the Hawaii Karate Congress, which united nine clubs under its leadership. The purpose of this congress was to:

1. Aid in the establishment of an amiable relationship and unity among the membership.
2. Enhance the progress and advancement of karate through the study and guidance of the teachings of karate.
3. Propagate goodwill.
4. Aid in every way the advancement of the art of karate as a recognized sport, and to help develop a much higher degree of sportsmanship.[79]

A spokesman for this organization indicated that the congress was the first of its kind in the world to combine different *ryu* under one head.[80]

On November 5, 1961, the Hawaii Karate Congress sponsored a karate exhibition at the Honolulu Civic Auditorium featuring guest stars from Japan, including 10th-*dan* Kanki Izumikawa, 5th-*dan* Hidetaka Nishiyama of *Shotokan Karate,* and 4th-*dan* Hirokata Kanazawa, former All-Japan Shotokan Freestyle Champion. This array of Japanese stars dazzled the huge crowd at the Honolulu Civic, and was undoubtedly the single greatest motivation for increased karate activity since Chojun Miyagi's journey to the islands in 1934.

From 1961 to the present, karate has experienced a growth rate unrivaled in the United States by any other foreign art or sport. Since becoming our 50th state, Hawaii has evolved as a center of karate to the place that teams have been sent from Japan to compete with island talent, and on one occasion were roundly defeated by the Hawaiian team. The importance of Hawaii's role in karate development can no longer be disputed, since, with its more than one hundred *shodan* recipients, each capable of starting his own club, it can logically be looked on as the fountainhead of the truly amazing karate phenomenon.

*   *   *   *

The chronological development of Asian martial arts per se on the mainland United States has been rather cloudy. Earlier *ch'üan fa* practice in the Chinese community was discussed at length and was seen to be customarily practiced by none but the Chinese. However, in 1964, the restrictive doors of *ch'üan fu* were set ajar when Master Wong Ark-Yucy of Los Angeles, from China, opened his teachings to all races.[81] His Wah Que Chinese Kung-fu Studio in Los Angeles' Old Chinatown has been followed by several other *kung-fu (ch'üan fa)* studios in the greater Los Angeles area, most of which emphasize the health value of *kung-fu* exercise.

Karate, on the other hand, was virtually non-existent in the United States prior to the mid-1950's. From 1964 to 1966, over one hundred Okinawan-Americans in

17.   Wong Ark-yuey, master of *ch'üan fa* who is presently teaching in Los Angeles, California.

California were interviewed and none admitted to personal knowledge of the art, though most had a cursory familiarity with the term and what it represented. Although no evidence could be found of any local ongoing instruction in karate among the ranks of these people, there were several reports of individuals engaging in the practice before World War II. These stories centered around a Mr. Hokama and a Mr. Aragaki who were located in the Delano area of northern California in the 1930's.[82] However, neither of them was supposed to have maintained karate classes which leads us to the interesting fact that none of the people who have fostered California's karate "craze" claim Okinawan ancestry.

Why the lack of karate activity among California's Okinawans when it was the same type of immigrant who originated karate practice in Hawaii? The possible explanations are diverse.

The Okinawans interviewed may have been feigning ignorance of the subject so that they could maintain the traditional secrecy that formerly surrounded karate in the Ryukyus. But this supposition seems less likely when it is noted that no difficulty was experienced in communicating with the Okinawans who were responsible for karate's early beginnings in Hawaii. Since the Okinawan immigrants in the United States came from approximately the same areas of Okinawa, why would secrecy exist in California and not Hawaii? One possible answer is that Orientals as a whole were treated poorly in California from the mid-1800's on. This fact has led a large segment of the Oriental community to be only reluctantly communicative ever since. Thus, even in today's era of enlightened racial tolerance, Caucasians on the American mainland who try to delve deeply into the Asian "mystique" are often treated with suspicion by those who were forced to spend a segment of their lives in the ignominious "relocation" camps that sprang up in the western United States during World War II.

Aside from the above possibilities, there is the fact that California-bred Okinawans reside in scattered areas rather than in close-knit communities such as the Chinese were wont to form. The common tie of blood and ethnic practices was seemingly not enough to bring these scattered Okinawans together for participation in their endemic pastime. Suffice it to say that those Okinawans who did practice karate did so to the exclusion of all others, such that karate was virtually absent from the American mainland prior to 1953.

The United States Air Force, interested in Japanese martial arts since the close of World War II, in 1953 sponsored instruction for their personnel in judo and karate. Waseda, Keio, and Takushoku universities offered karate instructors for these special Air Force classes, and, later in that same year, Hidetaka Nishiyama led an Air Force sponsored tour of American air bases in the United States.[83] This tour, though limited to military installations, was the first broad introduction of karate to the American public.

The opening date of the first United States-based karate school is open to some speculation. With several hundred thousand service personnel having traveled to Okinawa and Japan between 1945 and the present, some karate-trained individuals undoubtedly began karate instruction in their own American hometowns after discharge from the military. But the first documented commercial karate school did not come from a former serviceman. Edward Parker of the Hawaiian Islands appears to have founded, in 1954, what is most likely the first commercially successful karate school in the United States. This took place in Provo, Utah, while Parker was obtaining his bachelor's degree in sociology at Brigham Young University.[84] Upon graduation he moved to Pasadena, California, where he opened his *kempo-karate* school in 1956. Here again the semantics of the terms "kempo" and "karate" come into focus. Edward Parker received his *shodan* from the formerly mentioned Mitose graduate, William Chow. Although Parker took additional training in other weaponless arts, he credits his fundamental style of self-defense to Chow. While Parker is called an instructor of karate, he leans heavily toward the philosophical tradition of James Mitose's *Kosho-ryu Kempo*. Thus, if Dr. Mitose's statement and personal conviction is true that *kempo* is intrinsically different from karate, we must conclude that Parker is not a karate instructor in the Okinawan sense; but that nevertheless his hybrid "karate-kempo-ju-jutsu, etc." is equally as effective in its fighting aspects as any of the purely Okinawan styles being performed today.

Edward Parker's martial art prominence has resulted in his being engaged to teach a number of famous people, many of whom are from the film industry such as Elvis Presley, Blake Edwards, Robert Culp, etc. He has also appeared in several episodes of the successful television series "I Spy" as one of the "heavies," using his *karate-kempo* to villainous ends.

The first "pure" style of karate was introduced to the United States mainland in 1956 by a Japanese national named Tsutomu Ohshima who opened his school of Shotokan Karate in Los Angeles.[85] In 1959 Ohshima taught his arts in Brazil and France, finally returning to Japan in 1960. After some time had passed, Ohshima arranged for the well-known Hidetaka Nishiyama to come to California to supervise his Shotokan Karate School until he could return personally in 1963. After Ohshima returned Mr. Nishiyama branched off to form his own club. These two men could be called the germinal influence for "pure" karate's great popularity in America today, and combined they presently head an impressive list of karate experts residing in the United States.

After 1959 the United States "karate explosion" began in earnest. But because until now there has been no organization to speak of, there has arisen an enormous number of weaponless martial arts schools, some of which bear little resemblance to their Oriental ancestors. This unfortunate circumstance has triggered a similar degeneration of the original arts in Canada, Europe, and even in parts of the Asian world. The fact that on the mainland United States, California is no longer the sole repository of karate is attested to by the American directory of karate schools listed monthly in a popular martial arts publication. At one time the list was as follows:

Arizona 2, California 34, Colorado 2, Connecticut 2, Florida 1, Georgia 2, Hawaii 6, Illinois 7, Indiana 4, Iowa 1, Kentucky 1, Louisiana 1, Maryland 2, Massachusetts 3, Mississippi 1, Missouri 4, Nebraska 1, New Jersey 9, New York 16, North Carolina 1, Oklahoma 1, Oregon 1, Pennsylvania 7, Rhode Island 3, South Carolina 1, Tennessee 3, Texas 5, Utah 1, Virginia 1, Washington 2, Washington D.C. 1, Wisconsin 1, and the Territory of Guam 1.[86]

This total of one-hundred twenty-eight karate schools sounds impressive, but the fact is even more impressive when it is realized that this figure represents, by conservative estimate, but one-third of the existing schools in the United States. Thus, the author estimates that from the handful of weaponless martial arts participants of the 1950–1960 era, there will be well over a quarter of a million participants by the end of the present decade, and that karate training will soon be included in the nation's basic physical education curriculum, as well as becoming an integral part of American amateur athletics. Truly can karate be ranked among the United States' remarkable space-age phenomena!

Chapter 9

Karate and the Law

AT ITS "grass roots" level, law enforcement by its very nature involves a great deal of physical activity. Much of this activity finds the individual police officer pitted directly against the offender or the suspected offender. Thus, it goes without saying that as a professional group, policemen are more intensely concerned with hand-to-hand combat skills than any other civilian organization. They must, then, devote a serious part of their training to the learning of combat skills that will enable them to handle virtually any violent situation that arises with the greatest dispatch, both for self-preservation, for the sake of effective follow-through in situations they feel inclined to move on, and to protect the nearby general public from becoming involved in an uncontrolled melee.

There is a fourth consideration in contemporary law enforcement circles that a substantial part of the police man's job is of a quasi-public relations nature. That is to say, he is trying to lose the stigma of the heavy-handed, mutton-headed "cop" of yore into the almost genteel, diplomatic servant-of-the-people who is capable of preventing crime in as innocuous a manner as possible. Of course, in so conducting themselves, they are also able to categorize themselves as "professional" men, and as such, command better salaries then their "laboring" group contemporaries. Thus it can be seen that there are many reasons for policemen to improve their weaponless combat skills as well as the many other skills that they are called upon to know and use effectively.

Thus far there has not been found one fighting technique that suffices for all possible emergency situations, though many have been tried and are being used today.

A number of self-defense styles have been experimented with and are sometimes adopted in part, but until now have never been seized upon as the "answer" to the need.

Yawara, an ancient Japanese leverage technique (see Chapter Six), was used experimentally by the Berkeley, California, Police Department under the direction of the late Frank Matsuyama. However, according to a 1966 letter from Berkeley Police Chief A. H. Fording, its usefulness was quite limited for the reasons stated herein:

This department has not been involved in the teaching of yawara for nearly twenty-five years. We were never completely satisfied with it for two basic reasons. First, it was hazardous to our own personnel during the instructional period and we had a number of men seriously injured, some permanently. Second, like so many systems which depend upon leverage, we found that it was hazardous to persons with whom we were dealing. In other words, it was too easy to seriously injure an individual when overcoming some opposition or resistance.

At the present time our officers are given a self-defense course which is based primarily upon judo with some modifications as developed by the U.S. military services. It consists primarily of a few simple throws, holds, come-alongs, breaks, and defense against weapons. We have never utilized karate.

18.   Members of the Los Angeles County Sheriff's Department in California practice weaponless combat drills. *Courtesy of the Los Angeles County Sheriff's Department.*

Yawara is certainly one of the most exotic of the Asian martial arts to be given a trial in the United States. Such use indicates the extent to which police departments have been going in their search for improved methods.

The "sit-in" tactic of the civil rights movement and Vietnam protest groups in the United States have brought a new and different task to law enforcement. Officers are now called upon to move bodily great numbers of people who have been specially trained to resist arrest by sitting, squatting, or lying limply in a dead-weighted position. The problem is compounded by onlookers who regularly jump in and try to prevent the police from carting the bodies to police vans. But after learning a few simple ju-jutsu and judo techniques, the police have been able to move these people with a minimum of violence and with much greater alacrity. In its great preoccupation with bodily leverage, judo had been found to be a "goldmine" in working out methods for seizing, taking down, and for the much-used police "come-along" holds that are so extensively utilized by police agencies the world over.

Aside from the civil disobedience and non-violence problems associated with 20th-century America, there looms on the law enforcement horizon a threat entirely overlooked by police agencies in this country. This problem is the "karate phenomenon." Karate as an effective fighting art, becomes even deadlier in the hands of many Americans. This is so because very few teachers of this art have taken the time to emphasize the all-important moral training in conjunction with their martial arts skills. As a result, few karate practitioners have learned that there is a code of ethics that is as strict as the karate techniques are strong. The presently heavy accent of *kumite* (free style matches) and street-fighting techniques can be likened to the inclusion of hair-triggered firearms in the toyboxes of children. In an American society that is undergoing a not too subtle change, contemporary themes are speaking out that are seldom non-violent. What with the rising voice of "Black Power" versus the militant status quo attitude of many "whites" throughout the nation, all forms of violence and particularly the phenomenon of karate becomes a serious potential threat to peace, especially when one hears of certain "Black" nationalist organizations (e.g., Black Muslims) having karate trained "enforcers."[1]

Interested in law enforcement's attitude toward karate in the United States the author queried twenty-six American cities where karate is practiced in schools or clubs to see if they had formulated a policy concerning the study and application of karate, and also if any of their officers were given special instruction either in karate-associated skills or in defense against an aggressor who is using karate. The results of this questionnaire are incorporated into the chart on the following page.

1. Our police department is familiar with karate and its various techniques.
2. The department inspects karate schools in the city for safety measures.
3. Minors are allowed to practice karate without special permission of the police department.
4. There is a regular program where officers learn karate or defense against it.
5. Karate schools teaching the art are licensed by city ordinance.
6. There has been a police officer of this city injured by a suspect using karate.
7. A person using karate in this city would be guilty of attack with a deadly weapon; hence, felonious assault.

City Police Dept.	1.	2.	3.	4.	5.	6.	7.
Atlanta, Ga.	Yes	No	Yes	Yes	Yes	?	No
Birmingham, Ala.	Yes	No	?	No	No	No	Yes
Buffalo, N.Y.	Yes	No	Yes	Yes	No	No	*
Chicago, Ill.	Yes	No	Yes	No	No	No	Yes
Denver, Colo.	Yes	No	Yes	Yes	Yes	No	*
Des Moines, Iowa	Yes	No	?	No	?	No	?
Detroit, Mich.	Yes	No	Yes	Yes	No	No	No
Eugene, Ore.	Yes	No	Yes	Yes	No	No	*
Evanston, Ill.	Yes	No	Yes	No	No	No	*
Fort Worth, Tex.	Yes	No	Yes	Yes	Yes	No	*
Honolulu, Hawaii	Yes	No	Yes	Yes	No	No	No
Indianapolis, Ind.	Yes	No	?	No	Yes	No	*
Jackson, Miss.	Yes	No	?	Yes	No	No	Yes
Kansas City, Mo.	No	No	Yes	No	Yes	No	*
Los Angeles, Calif.	Yes	No	Yes	Yes	Yes	No	*
Miami, Florida	Yes	No	Yes	No	Yes	No	Yes
Minneapolis, Minn.	Yes	No	Yes	Yes	No	**	No
Oklahoma City, Okla.	Yes	No	?	Yes	Yes	No	Yes
Philadelphia, Penn.	Yes	No	Yes	No	Yes	No	*
Phoenix, Ariz.	Yes	No	Yes	No	Yes	No	Yes
Pittsburg, Penn.	No	No	?	No	Yes	Yes	*
Portland, Ore.	Yes	No	?	Yes	Yes	No	*
Raleigh, N.C.	Yes	No	No	No	Yes	No	Yes
Rochester, N.Y.	Yes	No	Yes	No	No	No	Yes
St. Louis, Mo.	Yes	No	Yes	Yes	Yes	No	Yes
Tacoma, Wash.	Yes	No	?	No	Yes	No	*

* Depends on circumstances.
** In training.

Please note that in a number of cities (e.g., Fort Worth, Detroit, Oklahoma City, Jackson, St. Louis, Minneapolis, Denver, Los Angeles, Buffalo, Atlanta, Eugene, Portland, and Honolulu) the reporting agencies have initiated special training sessions devoted specifically to handling one's self in situations where the suspect is utilizing karate, or karate-like, skills in avoiding arrest. The St. Louis, Missouri, Police Department, in fact, teaches Shorin-ryu karate to all officer candidates.[2] The Honolulu Police Department, on the other hand, noting the tremendous growth in karate, has offered classes to its officers in defense *against* karate. Police Chief Dan Liu himself is a karate student with Honolulu instructor Edward "Bobby" Lowe.

The State of Hawaii has also pioneered in giving karate instruction to the guards in its penal institutions. Ray Belnap, Director of the Hawaii State Correctional System, introduced karate and judo to his guards several years ago, and has developed his system until today nearly a hundred of the State Prison security personnel are engaged in the learning of some phases of these skills.[3]

Few cases of assault in which the offender used karate techniques have been noted publicly. However, incidents are known where persons using karate severely injured their non-practitioning opponent, and the details of the incident were not reported to the investigating authorities. Also, of the twenty-six cities queried, Pittsburg had the only police agency that reported an officer injured by a karate-trained suspect. This and other fragmentary reports of karate being used offensively poses the legal question that has been faced by many Asian police agencies: can the "karate arts" be considered a "weapon" in the sense that their use would constitute an aggravated crime such as felonious assault? The answers given by the twenty-six law enforcement agencies vary greatly. That this question must be answered is obvious; and the mere fact that the question is now being asked is indication that karate holds a unique position in American society. Law enforcement must take a careful look at the karate-like arts and, together with the legislative bodies, help to enact laws that protect both officer and untrained citizen alike.

There is a popular belief in the United States that karate enthusiasts must "register" their hands as dangerous weapons with the local police. At the time of this writing, it can be asserted unequivocally that this is nothing more than a modern myth. In fact, as far as could be ascertained, there were no restrictions on karate practitioners that even approached those levied against boxers and wrestlers. As for the qualifications to teach karate, the only requirement needed to open one's own school is a simple business license. Therefore, there is absolutely no guarantee that the karate school in one's neighborhood is not rife with unscrupulous "toughs" whose greatest pleasure is to test their newly acquired "skills" on innocent passers-by. Law enforcement agencies, of course, are not legislative bodies nor are they engaged in the business of licensing. However, they do have more power than merely to enforce laws already on the statutes and to apprehend known criminals in that they can recommend needed legislation. And it seems apparent that such recommendations are better forthcoming early in the development of a potential problem rather than after it has grown into a giant. Yet, if past patterns are repeated, painful experience may be the only alternative to tighter legal restrictions concerning karate and the law.

Chapter 10

Modern Trends

A MAN IN his late twenties sauntered along a dirt road in rural Japan, his springy step and cheerful attitude belied the ten hours he had just spent tilling the muddy earth in preparation for the June rice planting. His karate *gi* was carefully tucked into a worn vinyl bag which he carried casually over his left shoulder. Although his posture was relaxed, the man's overall appearance was one of self-assurance, a natural consequence of his having attained the *san-dan* rank after six grueling years of training. The wind threatening rain from the southeast hurried him along; he wanted a full three hours of training—from seven to ten—before the long walk home.

While this introduction might well be the beginning of a fictional narrative or a scenario for a film, it is in fact a true account. The moral of the brief anecdote is that dedication is necessary before a mere series of physical accomplishments becomes a true "art." The little story further illustrates that there are still persons in the world who cling to the almost "medieval" philosophy that total devotion to a skill or idea is a necessary experience for developing the "whole man."

Martial arts training in Japan exists for the most part on a completely different level than in the United States.

19. Tenri University (Kyoto) students engage in traditional board-punching exercise to train the knuckles. This form of training, called *makiwara*, often results in injured and even broken fingers. *Photograph by Akio Inoue.*

However, the author will frankly admit that not all of the karate enthusiasts in Japan are like our young farmer friend. In fact, Japan has more than her share of dilettantes and quasi-*bu-jutsu* men. There is even found a rather pronounced interest in karate by Japan's criminal element—an unfortunate degradation of the art that has largely occurred since the end of World War II—such that karate-trained bodyguards and "strong men" are rather common in the Japanese underworld.

Taken overall, however, karate and most of the other

20.   While the lack of snow may not make it evident, the students of Tenri University are practicing here in winter on frosted sod, displaying their devotion to karate. Bare feet is traditional. *Photograph by Akio Inoue.*

Japanese *bu-jutsu* have had a dynamically positive impact on the culture of these islands.

In comparing martial arts development in the United States with that of Japan, then, the thing that seems not to have accompanied karate, judo, kendo, and aikido on their long voyage eastward is this concept of devotion. An advertisement in one of the commonly read American men's magazines indicates how most individuals in this country approach the study of karate:

I'll make you a master of karate. The results of hundreds of years of development in Japan, karate is the secret, Oriental art of deadly self-defense that turns your hands, arms, legs into paralyzing weapons. . . . In just two hours after you receive "Super Karate" you will be on your way to being an invincible karate master. . . .[1]

The panacea for the perennial ninety-seven pound weakling of the 1940's was judo or jiu-jitsu, the first mail-order do-it-yourself bubble. Those currently in search of "instant self-confidence" look to karate for their "salvation," seeing the art in its brutal aspects, but generally overlooking the basics of karate in its totality. Granted, we have shown in Chapter Seven that karate's interconnection with the time-honored practices of Taoism and Buddhism is in most cases superficial. Still, because of the way in which Gichin Funakoshi introduced the art to Japan, there is enough of a philosophical heritage in karate practice to enable one to look upon it as more than an exceptionally effective military skill. For Funakoshi was primarily an educator, a former normal-school teacher on Okinawa, who saw in karate the vehicle for educating the whole man—body, mind, and spirit. He was a tireless disciplinarian as well as a master of karate. His emphasis on the moral ethics of karate and his refusal to teach the art to the lay public—he instructed only military and college personnel—resulted in karate's rather emphatic acceptance into the time-honored family of the Japanese martial arts.[2]

The evolvement of karate in Japan has followed two general patterns. Those Okinawan instructors who came first (e.g., Funakoshi, Miyagi, etc.) to teach their skills at a university or college established the mode for achieving the greatest advancement in the art. The largest number of karate students in present-day Japan have emerged from the hallowed institutions of higher learning. These karate practitioners have elevated karate to a plateau rivaling judo, no mean accomplishment when one realizes that judo is commonly thought of by some Japanese and foreigners alike to be Japan's national pastime.

The other developmental trend in karate grew from those instructors from Okinawa who did not affiliate themselves with a university. Needing a livelihood, these men opened karate schools to anyone with the prescribed fee of instruction. The gangster elements using karate today have emerged from the instructor who has had to admit "all-comers" in order to make financial ends meet.

We have a reversal of this position in contemporary American karate, where only one instance of karate study for credit is known to have been added to a college's physical education curriculum. In September, 1964, the California Institute of Technology in Pasadena, California, under the tutelage of Shotokan expert Tsutomu Ohshima, began regular course instruction in karate. Ohshima *sensei* actually began karate instruction at Caltech in an unofficial capacity as early as 1958, when he formed one of the first college karate clubs in the United States.

The University of California at Los Angeles' Department of Education, noting the vigorous physical training methods used in karate, began a study of comparative anatomical strengths of karate practitioners and college wrestlers. The results indicated that, whereas the karate-men were about on a par with the college athletes in the areas of back strength, left-hand grip, and right-hand grip, they were far superior in comparative leg strength.[3]

In present-day America at least 95 per cent of the functioning karate schools are "open," in that all persons are welcome to seek training. In many such schools the tactics of the now-defunct fly-by-night weight lifting gymnasiums are used to get signatures on contracts that bind the student to a designated number of lessons for rather elaborate fees. These schools, run solely for profit, are especially guilty of improper screening of new applicants. On the other hand, there are schools which operate strictly as "clubs" and which are non-profit in orientation. These, for the most part, have some sort of screening process for student candidates. Yet in too many instances they are guilty of teaching karate to undesirables as well. The sobering aspect of the picture of American karate is that there are thousands of potentially dangerous individuals being produced annually in the United States. The United States has not the moral or the socially developed concept of her people living peacefully together, a fact keenly observed by many social scientists who in turn marvel at the Japanese ability to live together in extremely crowded conditions in near perfect harmony.

Like the sudden appearance of Zen Buddhism in the late 1950's, karate has burst on the American cultural scene; but also, like Zen, the karate crescendo will surely diminish in due time because of the lack of control with which it has been developing. It has all but lost its identity and is at the time of this writing little more than a "bandwagon" onto which nearly every imaginable Eastern fighting art form has jumped and is clinging precariously. Occasionally, however, one of the karate-like arts remains out of the karate camp, and has succeeded in achieving an identity of its own. For example, T'ai Chi Ch'üan, an esoteric form of *ch'üan fa* (see Chapters Three and Eight), is being taught in the form of "body awareness." In the Big Sur area of California, long noted as a center for avant-garde cultural activities, T'ai Chi instructor Gia-Fu Feng is working for nonverbal communication through "meditation-in-action."[4] Feng's group is in many ways similar to the Zen study groups of the last decade, and his success seems to imply that there is a place for the Asian arts in American society so long as they are presented in their undiluted ("pure") or original form.

Yet, karate in America is still by and large identified with brick-breaking and the often brutal free-style *(kumite)* competitions that comprise nearly every tournament presented in the United States. The true bases of the art (i.e., *kata,* breathing-exercises, and achieving harmony with one's higher nature) are all but forgotten aspects. With television and motion picture writers exploiting every sensational aspect of karate and, as always, adding a few gimmicks of their own, it is small wonder that the public views the karate-like arts as they do.

The rather haphazard growth of American karate since 1958 has prompted many of its leading figures to attempt formation of a nationwide karate association which would mediate the incessant problems that loom large on the American karate horizon. The aforementioned Tsutomu Ohshima, who pioneered "pure" Shotokan style in continental United States, and who made his American teaching debut in 1956, is among those desiring such an association, as is *kempo-karate* businessman-actor-instructor Ed Parker who also opened his California school in 1956. Ohshima and Parker are joined at present by Korean karate expert Jhoon Rhee and U.S. Senator Milton Young, also an avid karate student (see *Life* magazine, May 20, 1966), in their attempt to unite karate factions and to fuse karate into American amateur athletics.[5] The tangible reward for their efforts, it is hoped, will be recog-

21. *Kumite* or free-style contests are popular aspects in Japanese karate tournaments. *Courtesy of Doshisha University (Kyoto) Karate Club.*

22.   The power of karate is graphically illustrated, as a Tenri University student executes *tameshiwari* (tile breaking). The faces of the holders are covered to protect them from flying tile splinters. *Photograph by Akio Inoue.*

nition and official sanction by the Amateur Athletic Union (AAU).

Indicative of the confused American karate picture is the fact that there are two other organizations that are hopeful of gaining AAU recognition as the authoritative karate society in the United States. Hidetaka Nishiyama of Shotokan Karate has long been interested in heading a nationwide organization of karate practitioners, and has worked toward that end ever since his initial appearance in this country as a touring karate expert for the U.S. Air Force in 1953. Nishiyama now heads the All-America Karate Association (AAKA) in Los Angeles, an affiliate of the powerful All Japan Karate Association.[6] While Nishiyama's credentials as a bonafide master of the art are unimpeachable, his Japanese citizenship and his difficulty with the English language have thus far hindered his acceptance by the AAU as the person to lead a politically oriented American karate federation.

The third known individual interested in heading a nationwide karate federation is Robert Trias, who presently directs a collection of karate schools called the United States Karate Association (USKA) which is based in Arizona.[7]

Combined with this interesting battle to the karate throne in the United States is the difficulty arising from the fact that many of the presently active karate organizations refuse to recognize each others' credentials. This is particularly true of groups headed by Japanese-born instructors, many of whom disdain all schools created by "instructors" who obtained degrees in other than true Okinawan styles. And, even among so-called "legitimate" schools of Okinawan karate, there are petty jealousies which have hurt the chance for total unification.

In the state of Hawaii is found the greatest concentration of karate adherents and diversification of karate styles. However, Hawaii as a whole has shown little interest in courting any of the three U.S. mainland organizations now vying for AAU recognition because of its own well-established Hawaii Karate Congress (HKC). Both because the HKC is the oldest karate organization in the U.S.,[8] and because Hawaii is still quite isolated from the rest of the United States, this reluctance to be absorbed is certainly understandable. Moreover, except for select individuals, Hawaiian karate enthusiasts think poorly of mainland American karate in general. This feeling stems largely from the fact that the majority of instructors in the HKC have been trained in Japan or Okinawa with the extreme rigors that such training implies. Thus they cannot but feel that the "90-day wonder" black belts found in many mainland schools are a travesty to their art, and thus want no part of them. It presently appears that Hawaii will continue a "go-it-alone" policy in terms of national federations and power-elite organizations.

It is interesting to note also that disharmony reigns even in Japan. Because of the rivalries that have existed between the various *ryu* since karate's formative years on Okinawa, it seems unlikely that the approximately one million students of karate in Japan will ever fall neatly into permanent unification. But a positive sign of forward-moving steps is the recent consolidation, albeit a temporary one, of the top four styles, *Wado-ryu, Shito-ryu, Goju-ryu, and Shotokan-ryu.*[9]

It has been estimated that approximately seven to ten thousand Americans have had karate training of some form since the end of World War II. This estimate naturally leaves one with the question, where is karate going in the United States? Perhaps a data-computing machine programmed with tidbits of information concerning karate as an art, a sport, a means of self-defense; the psychological reasons for karate study; the sociological environment of its practitioners; and the general outcome of most fads, Asian and non-Asian, would enable sociologists to arrive at a fairly accurate prediction. It is logical, that if American karate grows at the same rate that it did in Japan, we should, by the turn of the century, have over two million active participants, and nearly five million who had some contact with karate during their lives. As it is, karate has blossomed with rather fantastic profusion in this country. And even if the schools and the instructors are somewhat less devoted than their Japanese and Okinawan counterparts, the interest does exist, and there is every likelihood that it will burgeon for some time to come. Karate instructor Tsutomu Ohshima told the author that if one hundred karate students in America are genuine and honest in their study—in spite of the "phonies" and the "charlatans"—then karate practice in this country is valid and good. History will be the judge of Ohshima *sensei*'s words.

Notes & Sources

Chapter 1 Introduction & Terminology
1. Pu Chen-chie, *Kuo Chih Chien Luen* (Shanghai, 1936), pp. 12–13.
2. Gichin Funakoshi, *Karate-jutsu* (Tokyo, 1925), p. 3.
3. Masatatsu Oyama, *What Is Karate?* (Tokyo, 1958), p. 29.
4. Hirokata Toyama, *Karate-do* (Tokyo, 1958), p. 23.
5. *Ibid.,* p. 24.
6. *Ibid.*
7. *Ibid.*
8. *Ibid.*
9. Hironori Otsuka, *Sekai Dai-Hyakkajiten,* VI (Tokyo, 1955), p. 213.

Chapter 2 India
1. William Soothill, *The Lotus of the Wonderful Law* (Oxford, 1930), p. 181.
2. *Fa Hua San Ch'ing* (Shanghai, 1921), p. 2 of Chapter XIV.
3. William Soothill, *Dictionary of Chinese Buddhist Terms* (London, 1932). The ideography 那羅 are read as *nalo* [nah-low] in Mandarin, a transliteration of the Sanskrit *nata*.
4. *Ibid.*
5. Yasuhiro Konishi, *Karate Nyumon* (Tokyo, 1958), p. 216. The famous karate master feels that *nata* is a definite link between early Indian fighting and modern karate.
6. *Hongyo-kyo* is the popular name for the *Busshogyosan* or *Buddhacarita-karya Sutra* in Sanskrit. Its Chinese name is

Pen-hsing Ch'ing and the original author is unknown, but the work seems to have been written *ca.* 424–453, according to the definitive Japanese Buddhist reference entitled *Bussho Kaisetsu Daijiten.*

7. Konishi, *op. cit.*
8. Sir Monier Monier-Williams, *Sanskrit-English Dictionary* (Oxford, 1889), pp. 793–913.
9. Konishi, *Karate Nyumon,* p. 216.
10. Konishi, *Yasashii Karate No Narai Kata* (Tokyo, 1957), p. 13.
11. Konishi, *op. cit.,* p. 216.
12. Robert Paine and Alexander Soper, *The Art and Architecture of Japan* (Baltimore, 1955), p. 17.

Chapter 3   China

1. D. T. Suzuki, *The Essentials of Zen Buddhism* (New York, 1962), p. 106.
2. Kenneth Ch'en, *Buddhism in China* (Princeton, 1964), p. 351.
3. Hideo Nakamura, *Sekai Dai-Hyakkajiten,* XVIII (Tokyo, 1955), pp. 487–88.
4. Chou Hsiang-kuang, *A History of Chinese Buddhism* (Allahabad, India, 1955), p. 91.
5. Chou Hsiang-kuang, *Dhyana Buddhism, Its History & Teaching* (Allahabad, 1960), p. 20.
6. E. T. C. Werner, *A Dictionary of Chinese Mythology* (New York, 1961), p. 359.
7. Chou, *A History of Chinese Buddhism,* p. 91.
8. Suzuki, *op. cit.,* p. 109.
9. Ch'en, *op. cit.,* p. 352.
10. *Ibid.*
11. *Ibid.*
12. *Ibid.*
13. Chou, *Dhyana Buddhism . . . ,* pp. 20–21.
14. Suzuki, *op. cit.,* p. 117.
15. Ch'en, *op. cit.,* p. 352.
16. *Ibid.,* pp. 483–84.
17. Pierre Huard and Ming Wong, *La Medecine Chinoise Au Cours Des Siécles* (Paris, 1959), p. 173.
18. Werner, *op. cit.,* p. 260.

19. *Ibid.,* p. 268.
20. *Ibid.*
21. Huard and Ming, *op. cit.;* also, Pu Chen-chie, *op. cit.,* pp. 12–13; K. Chimin Wong and Wu Lien-teh, *History of Chinese Medicine, Being a Chronicle of Medieval Happenings in China from Ancient Times to the Present Period* (Shanghai, 1936), pp. 72–73.
22. Monier-Williams, *op. cit.,* p. 1889.
23. Konishi, *Yasashii Karate . . . ,* p. 13.
24. Pu, *op. cit.,* p. 13.
25. *Ibid.*
26. *Ibid.,* p. 13.
27. *Ibid.*
28. *Ibid.*
29. Konishi, *Yasashii Karate . . . ,* p. 17.
30. Pu, *op. cit.,* p. 14.
31. *Ibid.*
32. *Ibid.*
33. *Ibid.*
34. Werner, *op. cit.,* p. 360.
35. Chou, *Dhyana Buddhism . . . ,* p. 23.
36. Werner, *op. cit.*
37. Chou, *Dhyana Buddhism . . . ,* p. 23.
38. Werner, *op. cit.*
39. *Ibid.*
40. Konishi, *Yasashii Karate . . . ,* p. 16.
41. Carl Glick and Hong Sheng-Hwa, *Swords of Silence: Chinese Secret Societies Past and Present* (New York, 1947), p. 34.
42. *Ibid.*
43. Kenneth Scott Latourette, *A Short History of the Far East* (New York, 1959), p. 372.
44. Li Chien-nung, *Political History of China: 1840–1928* (London, 1956), p. 165.
45. *Ibid.*
46. *Ibid.*
47. "The Boxer Rebellion," adapted from the October, 1900, edition of the *Shanghai Mercury Newspaper,* p. 1.
48. Li, *op. cit.,* p. 177.

Chapter 4 Southeast Asia

1. W. Robert Moore, "Angkor, Jewel of the Jungle," *National Geographic Magazine* (April, 1960), pp. 518, 542.
2. *Ibid.,* p. 524.
3. *Ibid.,* p. 542.
4. Letter from W. Robert Moore, Chief Foreign Editorial Staff, *National Geographic Magazine* (November 15, 1965).
5. *Ibid.*
6. Moore article, p. 524.
7. *Ibid.*
8. George M. Kahin, ed. *Governments and Politics of South-East Asia,* second edition (New York, 1964), p. 597.
9. *Colliers Encyclopedia,* II (New York, 1961), p. 533.
10. Kahin, *op. cit.,* p. 375.
11. D.G.E. Hall, *A History of South-East Asia* (London, 1960), p. 170.
12. *Ibid.*
13. Peter T. White, "Saigon: Eye of the Storm," *National Geographic Magazine* (June, 1965), p. 870.
14. Kahin, *op. cit.,* p. 375.
15. *Ibid.,* p. 184.
16. *Ibid.*
17. Interview with Rudy Ter Linden and Paul De Thouars, Dutch-Indonesian *pukulan* experts residing in Los Angeles, California, 1966.
18. *Ibid.*
19. *Ibid.*
20. Tape-recorded interview with Abdul Samat, *bersilat* expert, University of Malaya, Kuala Lumpur, Malaysia, 1966.
21. A.J.G. Papineau, *Kuala Lumpur-Papineau's Guide,* 3rd edition (Singapore, 1964), pp. 54–55.
22. *Ibid.*
23. *Ibid.*
24. *Ibid.*
25. Letter from Professor Wang Gungwu, Chairman, History Department, University of Malaya, January 28, 1966.

Chapter 5 Okinawa

1. George H. Kerr, *Okinawa, The History of an Island People* (Tokyo, 1958), p. 22.

2. *Ibid.*
3. *Ibid.*
4. *Ibid.*, p. 29
5. *Ibid.*
6. *Ibid.*, p. 27
7. *Ibid.*, p. 40
8. *Ibid.*, account following is from this source.
9. *Ibid.*
10. Yukitake Yashiro, *Kyoku Ikyohan Karate* (Tokyo, 1958), p. 23.
11. Reikichi Oya, *Karate No Narai Kata* (Tokyo, 1958), p. 23.
12. Hironori Otsuka, *Sekai Dai-Hyakkajiten,* VI (Tokyo, 1955), p. 213.
13. Funakoshi, *op cit.*, p. 5.
14. Oya, *op. cit.*, p. 8.
15. Kerr, *op. cit.*, p. 72.
16. *Ibid.*, p. 66.
17. *Ibid.*, p. 75.
18. Oya, *op. cit.*, p. 9.
19. Kerr, *op. cit.*, pp. 83–84.
20. *Ibid.*, p. 86.
21. *Ibid.*, pp. 89–90.
22. *Ibid.*
23. *Ibid.*, p. 217.
24. *Ibid.*, pp. 91–92.
25. Oya, *op. cit.*, p. 8.
26. Kerr, *op. cit.*, pp. 151 *ff.*, 157.
27. Funakoshi, *op. cit.*, p. 3.
28. Konishi, *Yasashii Karate. . .* , p. 18.
29. Yasaburo Shimonaka, *Nippon Dai-Hyakkajiten,* V. (Tokyo, 1932), pp. 551–52.
30. Funakoshi, *op cit.*, p. 3.
31. *Ibid.*
32. *Ibid.*, p. 5.
33. Oya, *op. cit.*, p. 13.
34. Bruce A. Haines, *Karate and Its Development in Hawaii to 1959* (Honolulu, 1962), p. 62.
35. Oya, *op. cit.*, p. 10.
36. Funakoshi, *op. cit.*, p. 4.
37. Shimonaka, *op. cit.*, pp. 551–52.

38. Konishi, *Yasashii Karate. . .*, p. 16.
39. Oya, *op. cit.,* p. 8.
40. Keishichi Ishiguro, *Karate Hayai Wakari* (Tokyo, 1958), p. 11.
41. Oya, *op. cit.,* p. 10.

Chapter 6 Japan
1. Konishi, *Karate Nyumon,* p. 219.
2. *Ibid.*
3. Edwin O. Reischauer, *Japan: Past and Present* (New York, 1946), p. 269.
4. George Sansom, *A History of Japan to 1334* (Stanford, 1958), p. 423.
5. Konishi, *Karate Nyumon,* p. 219.
6. Latourette, *op. cit.,* p. 199.
7. Desmond Robbins, "The Throw; The Blow; and The Know," *This Is Japan: 1958* (Tokyo, 1958), pp. 214–17.
8. Latourette, *op. cit.,* p. 209.
9. *Ibid.,* p. 213.
10. Shunzo Sakamaki, "Ch'en Yuan-pin," *Eminent Chinese of the Ch'ing Period,* Vol. I (Washington, 1943), pp. 106-7.
11. *Ibid.*
12. Oyama, *op. cit.,* p. 29.
13. Sakamaki, *op. cit.,* p. 107.
14. Reverend T. Lindsay and Jigoro Kano, "Jiu Jutsu, the Old Samurai Art of Fighting Without Weapons, "*Transactions of the Asiatic Society of Japan,* XVI (Yokohama, 1889), p. 197.
15. *Ibid.,* p. 193.
16. *Yoen Jiho Sha* (Okinawan newspaper printed in the Hawaiian Islands), May 1, 1934, p. 3.
17. *Ibid.*

Chapter 7 Buddhism & Karate
1. Yashiro, *op. cit.,* p. 25.
2. Alan Watts, *The Way of Zen* (New York, 1957), p. 70.
3. D.T. Suzuki, *Zen Buddhism* (New York, 1956), p. 290.
4. *Ibid.,* p. 289.
5. *Ibid.,* p. 53.
6. Watts, *op. cit.,* p. 86.

7. *Ibid.,* p. 87.
8. Konishi, *Yasashii Karate* . . . , p. 16.
9. *Ibid.*
10. Wolfram Eberhard, *History of China* (Berkeley, 1956), p. 142.
11. *Ibid.,* p. 111.
12. Pu, *op. cit.,* p. 13.
13. Li, *op. cit.,* p. 166.
14. Suzuki, *Zen Buddhism,* p. 288.

Chapter 8   Karate in the United States

1. *Colliers Encyclopedia,* XIX (New York, 1961), pp. 10–11.
2. Latourette, *op. cit.,* p. 386.
3. Gunther Barth, *Bitter Strength, A History of the Chinese in the United States, 1850–1870* (Cambridge, Massachusetts, 1964), p. 110.
4. *Ibid.,* p. 78.
5. *Ibid.,* p. 80.
6. *Ibid.,* 94–95.
7. *Ibid.*
8. *Ibid.,* p. 102.
9. *Ibid.*
10. Calvin Lee, *Chinatown, U.S.A.* (New York, 1965), p. 36.
11. Barth, *op. cit ,* p. 103.
12. *Ibid.*
13. *Ibid.*
14. *Ibid.,* p. 106.
15. Lee, *op. cit.,* p. 35.
16. Tan Lo, "Ket On Association," *Pan Pacific Magazine* (October-December 1937), p. 49.
17. Interview with Hin Sum Young, executive secretary of United Chinese Society, Honolulu, May 1962.
18. Chung Wo Au, "See Yap Benevolent Society," *Pan Pacific Magazine* (October-December 1937), p. 49.
19. Young interview.
20. *Ibid.*
21. Lee, *op. cit.,* p. 61.
22. Young interview.
23. Interview with Tinn Chan Lee, May 1962.
24. *Ibid.*

25. *Ibid.*
26. *Ibid.*
27. Kiyoshi Ikeda, *A Comparative Study of Mental Illness Differences Among Okinawan and Naichi Japanese in Hawaii* (Honolulu, 1955), p. 25.
28. *Ibid.*, p. 24.
29. *Ibid.*
30. Latourette, *op. cit.*, p. 530.
31. Ernest K. Wakukawa, *A History of the Japanese People in Hawaii* (Honolulu, 1938), p. 28.
32. Latourette, *op. cit.*, p. 530.
33. *Ibid.*
34. *Ibid.*
35. *Ibid.*
36. Wakukawa, *op. cit.*, p. 143.
37. *Ibid.*
38. Claude A. Buss, *The Far East* (New York, 1960), p. 376 *ff.*
39. Haines, *op. cit.*, p. 62.
40. *Ibid.*, p. 63.
41. *Ibid.*
42. *Jitsugyo No Hawai* (May 1927), p. 50.
43. Haines, *op. cit.*, p. 65.
44. *Ibid.*
45. *Ibid.*
46. *Ibid.*, p. 66.
47. *Ibid.*
48. *Ibid.*
49. *Ibid.*
50. *Ibid.*
51. *Ibid.*, p. 67.
52. *Ibid.*
53. *Ibid.*
54. Interview with Chinei Kinjo, editor of *Yoen Jiho Sha,* April 1959, May 1962.
55. *Ibid.*
56. *Yoen Jiho Sha,* May 1, 1934, p. 3.
57. *Ibid.*
58. *Yoen Jiho Sha,* May 29, 1934, p. 3.
59. Haines, *op. cit.*, p. 71.
60. *Ibid*

61. Interviews with Dr. James M. Mitose, Los Angeles, California, 1958–60, 1966.
62. *Ibid.*
63. *Ibid.*
64. *Ibid.*
65. *Ibid.*
66. James M. Mitose, *What Is Self-Defense?* (Honolulu, 1953), p. 6.
67. Mitose interviews.
68. Mitose, *op. cit.*, p. 4.
69. Mitose interviews.
70. Haines, *op. cit.*, p. 75.
71. *Ibid.*, p. 77.
72. *Ibid.*, p. 76.
73. *Ibid.*, pp. 78–79.
74. *Ibid.*, p. 81.
75. *Ibid.*
76. *Ibid.*, p. 82.
77. *Ibid.*, p. 83.
78. *Ibid.*
79. *Ibid.*, p. 89.
80. *Ibid.*, p. 90.
81. Interview with Wong Ark-Yuey, 1965–66.
82. Interview with Tsutomu Ohshima, Waseda University graduate and Shotokan Karate expert, Los Angeles, California, June 1966.
83. *Ibid.*
84. Interview with Edward Parker, Pasadena, California, 1958, May 1966.
85. Ohshima interview.
86. *Black Belt* magazine (June, 1965), pp. 60–62.

Chapter 9 Karate and the Law

1. *Life* magazine, May 31, 1963, pp. 24–25.
2. Questionnaire received from Robert L. Berton, director of Public Relations, City of St. Louis Police Department, April 1966.
3. Alf Pratte, "Prison Guards Get New Weapons: Karate and Judo," *Black Belt* magazine (August 1966), p. 15.

Chapter 10 Modern Trends

1. Cited in *Sir* magazine (February 1964), p. 63.
2. Interview with Ohshima, July 1966.
3. "Total Proportional Strength of Experienced Karate Students," *Physical Education Research Quarterly,* Vol. 34, No. 1 (March 1963), pp. 108–10.
4. *Los Angeles Times,* April 24, 1966, p. 1 of Section C.
5. "The Race for the AAU," *Black Belt* magazine (July 1966), p. 13.
6. *Ibid.,* p. 14.
7. *Ibid.*
8. *Ibid.,* p. 50.
9. Letter from the head of Karate Department, Nihon University, Tokyo, Japan, March 1966.

Bibliography

The bibliography is divided into the following categories: Primary Written Sources, General Written Works, Newspapers, Magazines, Interviews, Letters, Questionnaires, Theses, and Special Sources.

A. Primary Written Sources

Funakoshi, Gichin: *Karate-jutsu,* Tokyo, 1925
Harrison, Ernest J.: *Manual of Karate,* London, 1959
Konishi, Yasuhiro: *Karate-do Nyumon,* Tokyo, 1958
——: *Karate Nyumon,* Tokyo, 1958
——: *Yasashii Karate No Narai Kata,* Tokyo, 1957
Mitose, James M.: *What Is Self-Defense?,* Honolulu, 1953
Nishiyama, Hidetaka and Richard Brown: *Karate, the Art of Empty Hand Fighting,* Tokyo, 1960
Oya, Reikichi: *Karate No Narai Kata,* Tokyo, 1958
Oyama, Masatatsu: *What Is Karate?,* Tokyo, 1958
——: *What Is Karate?* (revised edition), Tokyo, 1959
Pu Chen Chie: *Kuo Chih Jien Luen,* Shanghai, 1936
Toyama, Hirokata: *Karate-do,* Tokyo, 1958
Yashiro, Yukitake: *Kyoku Ikyohan Karate,* Tokyo, 1958

B. General Written Works

Barth, Gunther: *Bitter Strength, A History of the Chinese in the United States, 1850–1870,* Massachusetts, 1964
Blakney, R. B.: *Tao Te Ching* (translation from the Chinese), New York, 1955
Borton, Hugh: *Japan,* New York, 1950
Buss, Claude A.: *The Far East,* New York, 1960

Ch'en, Kenneth: *Buddhism in China,* Princeton, 1964

Chou Hsiang-kuang: *A History of Chinese Buddhism,* Allahabad, India, 1955

——: *Dhyana Buddhism, Its History & Teaching,* Allahabad, 1960

Conze, Edward: *Buddhism,* Oxford, 1957

Creel, H. G.: *Chinese Thought, from Confucius to Mao Tse-tung,* New York, 1953

Dumoulin, Heinrich: *A History of Zen Buddhism,* New York, 1963

——: *The Development of Zen After the Sixth Patriarch in the Light of Mumonkan,* New York, 1953

Eberhard, Wolfram: *History of China,* Berkeley, 1956

Fa Hua San Ch'ing, Shanghai, 1936

Fang, Chao-ying: (ed.) *Eminent Chinese of the Ch'ing Period* (3 vols.), Washington, D.C., 1943

Fitzgerald, C. P.: *China, A Short Cultural History* (third edition), New York, 1965

Glick, Carl and Hong Sheng-Hwa: *Swords of Silence: Chinese Secret Societies Past and Present,* New York, 1947

Goodrich, L. Carrington: *A Short History of the Chinese People* (third edition), New York, 1959

Goshal, Kumar: *People of India,* New York, 1944

Hall, D. G. E.: *A History of South-East Asia,* London, 1960

Harrison, Ernest J.: *The Fighting Spirit of Japan,* London, 1913

Heibonsha: *Daijiten* (26 vols.), Tokyo, 1932

Huard, Pierre and Ming, Wong: *La Medecine Chinoise Au Cours Des Siécles,* Paris, 1959

Inouye, Kenkai: *Hokkekyo Kowa,* Tokyo, 1939

Ishiguro, Keishichi: *Karate Hayai Wakari,* Tokyo, 1958

Kahin, George M.: (ed.) *Governments and Politics of South-East Asia* (second edition), New York, 1964

Kerr, George H.: *Okinawa: A History of an Island Poeple,* Tokyo, 1958

Kuno, Takeshi: *Album of Japanese Prints: Kamakura Period,* Tokyo, 1932

Latourette, Kenneth S.: *A Short History of the Far East,* New York, 1959

Lee, Calvin: *Chinatown, U.S.A.,* New York, 1965

Li Chien-nung: *Political History of China: 1840–1928,* London, 1956

Lind, Andrew: *An Island Community,* Chicago, 1938

——: *Hawaii's Japanese,* New Jersey, 1946

Makiyama, Thomas H.: *The Techniques of Aikido,* Honolulu, 1960

Mochizuki, Shinkyo: (ed.) *Bukkyo Daijiten,* Tokyo, 1935

Monier-Williams, Sir Monier: *Sanskrit-English Dictionary,* London, 1898

Monumenta Nipponica (20 vols.), Tokyo, 1965

Natori, Yonosuke: *Mai-Chi-Shan Caves,* Tokyo, 1957

Ono, Genmyo: (ed.) *Bussho Kaisetsu Daijiten,* Tokyo, 1935

Pan Ku: *History of the Former Han Dynasty* (2 vols), translation from the Chinese by Homer H. Dubbs, Baltimore, 1938

Papineau, A. J. G.: *Kuala Lumpur—Papineau's Guide,* Singapore, 1964

Reischauer, Edwin O.: *Japan, Past and Present,* New York, 1946

Robbins, Desmond: "The Throw; The Blow; and The Know," *This Is Japan: 1958,* Tokyo, 1958

Sansom, George: *A History of Japan to 1334,* Stanford, 1958

Sargeant, J. A.: *Sumo: The Sport and the Tradition,* Tokyo, 1959

SCAP: *Political Reorientation of Japan,* Washington, D. C., 1943

Sekai Dai Hyakkajiten (31 vols.), Tokyo, 1955

Sen, Gertrude: *Pageant of India's History,* New York, 1948

Shimmura, Izuru: (ed.) *Kaihyo Sosho* (6 vols.), Tokyo, 1928

Shimonaka, Yasaburo: (ed.) *Dai Hyakkajiten* (27 vols.), Tokyo, 1932

——: *Shiseki Kaidai,* Tokyo, 1936

——: *Kokushi Jiten* (4 vols.), Tokyo, 1932

Soothill, William: *Dictionary of Chinese Buddhist Terms,* London, 1932

——: *The Lotus of the Wonderful Law,* Oxford, 1930

Soper, Alexander and Robert Paine: *Art and Architecture of Japan,* Baltimore, 1955

Suzuki, D. T.: *Essays in Zen Buddhism,* New York, 1956

——: *The Essentials of Zen Buddhism,* New York, 1962

——: *The Lankavatara Sutra,* London, 1932

Transactions of the Asiatic Society of Japan (first series, 50 vols.)

Wakukawa, Ernest K.: *A History of the Japanese People in Hawaii,* Honolulu, 1938

Watts, Alan W.: *The Way of Zen,* New York, 1957

Werner, E. T. C.: *A Dictionary of Chinese Mythology,* New York, 1961

Wong, K. Chimin and Wu Lien-teh: *History of Chinese Medicine, Being a Chronicle of Medieval Happenings in China from Ancient Times to the Present Period,* Shanghai, 1936

Zurcher, Erik: *Buddhism,* New York, 1962

——: *The Buddhist Conquest of China: The Spread and Adaptation of Buddhism in Early Medieval China,* Leiden, 1959

C. Newspapers

Shanghai Mercury News: "Boxer Rebellion," Shanghai, 1900

Honolulu Advertiser: Honolulu, 1933, 1934, 1959–1962

Honolulu Star Bulletin: Honolulu, 1959–1962

Los Angeles Times: Los Angeles, 1966

Nippu Jiji: Honolulu, 1933–1935

Yoen Jiho Sha: Koloa, Kauai (Hawaii), 1933–1935

D. Magazines

Asia Scene: January, 1959

Black Belt magazine : 1962–66

Jitsugyo No Hawai: May 1927 and January, February, June, July, September 1933

Life magazine : October 1947, May 1966

Look magazine : February 1961

National Geographic Magazine: 1960, 1964, 1965

Pan Pacific magazine : October-December 1937

Physical Education Research Quarterly: March 1963

E. Interviews

Bingo, Thomas: Karate instructor, 1959

Chow, William: *Kempo-Karate* instructor, 1955, 1959

De Thouars, Paul: Indonesian martial arts expert, 1965, 1966

Gill, Lorin: Program director, Palama Settlement, 1959

Hasegawa, Yoshio: Assistant Chief of Police, Honolulu, 1959

Higa Watoku: Okinawan immigrant and karate practitioner, 1959

Hu, William: *Ch'üan fa* instructor, 1959

Kanashiro, Dr. James Z.: Okinawan-American citizen, 1962

Kerr, George: Authority on Okinawa and author, 1958

Kim, Richard: Karate instructor, 1959

Kinjo, Chinei: Editor of Okinawan-American newspaper, 1959, 1962

Kobayashi, Mitsugi: Karate instructor, 1959

Kubo, Earl: Honolulu Police Department, 1962

Lee, Tinn Chan: *Ch'üan fa* instructor, 1962

Lowe, Edward: Karate instructor, 1959

Matsumoto, James: Karate student, 1959

Meyer, Robert: Physical director, Nuuanu YMCA, 1962

Mitose, Dr. James M.: *Kempo* instructor and author, 1958–1960, 1966

Miyasaki, George: Karate instructor, 1959, 1961

Miyashiro, Thomas : Karate instructor, 1962

Murakami, Kenneth: Karate instructor, 1959, 1961

Murasaki, Yoshio: Karate instructor, 1962

Ohshima, Tsutomu: Karate instructor, 1966

Okubo, Shungo: Executive secretary, Moiliili Community Association, 1962

Oshiro, Masaichi: Karate instructor, 1955, 1959

Parker, Edward: *Kempo-Karate* instructor, 1958, 1966

Shimomi, Carlton: Karate instructor, 1959

Ter Linden, Rudy: Indonesian martial arts expert, 1965, 1966

Teruya, Kiso: Okinawan-American resident of Hawaii, 1962

Wong Ark-yuey: *Ch'üan fa* instructor, 1965

Yamaguchi, Paul: Karate instructor, 1959

Young, Hin Sum: Executive secretary, United Chinese Society, 1962

Young, Thomas: *Kempo* instructor, 1959, 1962

F. Letters

Arika, Hitoshi: Doshisha University Karate Club, 1966

Fukuda, Tokushi: President, Kagoshima University, 1966

Fujimura, Toru: Head, Student Affairs, Ibaraki University, 1966

Furukawa, Noboru: Office of Student Personnel, Rikkyo University, 1966

Hasegawa, Shuji: Office of the President, Gumma University, 1966

178 BIBLIOGRAPHY

Inoue, Akio: Overseas Missions Department, Tenri University, 1965

Moore, W. Robert: Chief, Foreign Editorial Staff, *National Geographic Magazine,* 1965

Karate Dobu: Nihon University, 1966

Karate Dobu: Tohoku University, 1966

Wang Gungwu: Head, Department of History, University of Malaya, 1966

G. Questionnaires

(Police Departments)

Atlanta (Georgia): Lt. R. M. Lane, Training Division

Birmingham (Alabama): Capt. Jack A. Warren, Personnel and Training

Buffalo (New York): Sgt. James H. Goss, Assistant Police Instructor

Chicago (Illinois): Robert E. McCann, Director of Training

Denver (Colorado): Lt. A. Dill, Director of Training

Des Moines (Iowa): Lt. B. B. Wallace

Detroit (Michigan): Lt. Bernard Winckoski

Eugene (Oregon): Lt. William W. Smith

Evanston (Illinois): Lt. Robert Witt, Planning and Research

Fort Worth (Texas): J. P. Moore, Planning Officer

Honolulu (Hawaii): Lt. Gladston Caringer, Planning and Training Division

Indianapolis (Indiana): Deputy Chief of Police O. K. Gleich

Jackson (Mississippi): Chief of Police W. D. Rayfield

Kansas City (Missouri): Lt. Marion L. Cooley, Planning and Research

Los Angeles (California): Lt. Ted Morton

Miami (Florida): Lt. Kenneth E. Fox

Minneapolis (Minnesota): Superintendent of Police Calvin F. Hawkinson

Oklahoma City (Oklahoma): Sgt. Lon L. Heggy, Planning and Research

Philadelphia (Pennsylvania): Capt. Michael Roxinon

Phoenix (Arizona): Sgt. B. Thompson, Public Information

Pittsburg (Pennsylvania): Sgt. E. A. Patterson, Personnel Division

Portland (Oregon): Lt. J. E. Harvey, Training Division

Raleigh (North Carolina): Lt. C. H. Haswell, Director of Personnel

Rochester (New York): Deputy Chief of Police Harry E. Griswald

St. Louis (Missouri): Robert L. Berton, Director of Public Relations

Tacoma (Washington): Police Department

H. Theses

Haines, Bruce A.: *Karate and Its Development in Hawaii to 1959,* University of Hawaii, 1962

Ikeda, Kiyoshi: *A Comparative Study of Mental Illness Differences Among Okinawan and Naichi Japanese in Hawaii,* University of Hawaii, 1955

Lin, Ronald: *Sunyata: Part II,* Ryukoku University (Kyoto, Japan), 1955

I. Special Sources

Film: "Paths of Nirvana"

Film: "Beyond the Great Wall"

Letter: Oyama to Edward Lowe, 1958

Tape Recorded Interview: *Bersilat* expert Abdhul Samat, from Dr. B. C. Stone, University of Malaya, 1966

Glossary-Index

181

"Put your hand inside the hat; search
with your fingers. He is the light
wrapped inside the darkness. That's the
wonder of Rabbit. We think he's not
in the hat. But he is."

~ *Samson Dupree*

TABLE OF CONTENTS

PROLOGUE

Have you ever wondered what happened to all those missing socks? Perhaps Harry and the Good Mischief Team have found the answer. There is an old New England tradition that tells of mysterious happenings at the stroke of midnight. According to custom, this was the time darkness had its way and when ghosts and witches flew—cloaking themselves in the shadows of night, flying their dark mischief, and wreaking havoc in the sky and town.

And this is the mystery in which Harry Moon found himself this time. Where do the missing socks go? Something dark had come to the Moon house. Something dark and indeed spooky.

FAMILY, FRIENDS & FOES

Harry Moon

Harry is the thirteen-year-old hero of Sleepy Hollow. He is a gifted magician who is learning to use his abilities and understand what it means to possess the real magic.

An unlikely hero, Harry is shorter than his classmates and has a shock of inky, black hair. He loves his family and his town. Along with his friend Rabbit, Harry is determined to bring Sleepy Hollow back to its true and wholesome glory.

Rabbit

Now you see him. Now you don't. Rabbit is Harry Moon's friend. Some see him. Most can't.

Rabbit is a large, black-and-white, lop-eared, Harlequin rabbit. As Harry has discovered, having a friend like Rabbit has its consequences. Never stingy with advice and counsel, Rabbit always has Harry's back as Harry battles the evil that has overtaken Sleepy Hollow.

Honey Moon

She's a ten-year-old, sassy spitfire. And she's Harry's little sister. Honey likes to say she goes where she is needed, and sometimes this takes her into the path of danger.

Honey never gives in and never gives up when it comes to righting a wrong. Honey always looks out for her friends. Honey does not like that her town has been plunged into a state of eternal Halloween and is even afraid of the evil she feels lurking all around. But if Honey has anything to say about it, evil will not be sticking around.

Samson Dupree

Samson is the enigmatic owner of the Sleepy Hollow Magic Shoppe. He is Harry's mentor and friend. When needed, Samson teaches Harry new tricks and helps him understand his gift of magic.

Samson arranged for Rabbit to become Harry's sidekick and friend. Samson is a timeless, eccentric man who wears purple robes, red slippers, and a gold crown. Sometimes, Samson shows up in mysterious ways. He even appeared to Harry's mother shortly after Harry's birth.

Mary Moon

Strong, fair, and spiritual, Mary Moon is Harry and Honey's mother. She is also mother to two-year-old Harvest. Mary is married to John Moon.

Mary is learning to understand Harry and his destiny. So far, she is doing a good job letting Harry and Honey fight life's battles. She's grateful that Rabbit has come alongside to support and counsel her. But like all moms, Mary often finds it difficult to let her children walk their own paths. Mary is a nurse at Sleepy Hollow Hospital.

John Moon

John is the dad. He's a bit of a nerd. He works as an IT professional and sometimes he thinks he would love it if his children followed in his footsteps. But he respects that Harry, Honey and possibly Harvest will need to go their own way. John owns a classic sports car he calls Emma.

Titus Kligore

Titus is the mayor's son. He is a bully of the first degree but also quite conflicted when it comes to Harry. The two have managed to forge a tentative friendship, although Titus will assert his bully strength on Harry from time to time.

Titus is big. He towers over Harry. But in a kind of David vs. Goliath way, Harry has learned which tools are best to counteract Titus's assaults while most of the Sleepy Hollow kids fear him. Titus would probably rather not be a bully but with a dad like Maximus Kligore he feels trapped in the role.

Maximus Kligore

The epitome of evil, nastiness, and greed, Maximus Kligore is the mayor of Sleepy Hollow. To bring in the cash, Maximus turned the town into the nightmarish, Halloween attraction it is today.

He commissions the evil-tinged celebrations in town. Maximus is planning to take Sleepy Hollow with him o Hell. But will he? He knows Harry Moon is a threat to his dastardly ways, but try as he might, he has yet to rid himself of Harry's meddling.

Kligore lives on Folly Farm and owns most of the town including the town newspaper.

THAT TERRIBLE PEACE

 All day and night, black town cars with dark, tinted windows crawled up and down the private driveway at Folly Farm. At the top of the hill, across from the tennis courts and swimming pool, smoke slithered into the night sky. At the edge of the estate, the We Drive By Night factory buzzed. This is where the latest and creepiest souvenirs, toys, and games were produced.

Harry Moon stood looking out his bedroom window. Sometimes, if the air was right, he could hear the clinging and clanging of the factory machines. He could always see the smoke that poured from the chimneys, and no matter how hard he tried, he always had the same sinking feeling. *Why couldn't I live in a normal town?*

Sleepy Hollow's mayor, Maximus Kligore, owned Folly Farm and pretty much every business concern in town including the highly profitable Chillie Willies, which sold scary paraphernalia all year long. But Chillie Willies was best known for the Halloween costumes they sold. Kligore had amassed a small fortune at the helm of Folly Farm, which he controlled with an iron fist.

Harry and his friends on the Good Mischief Team knew that beneath Kligore's ruthless management style lurked something much more sinister. The team, especially Harry, was convinced that Kligore had even greater and more terrible plans for their town. Harry had even seen Kligore, from time to time, dressed in a hooded, black cape wandering the town green and Shopper's Row late at night offering troubling curses.

As Harry watched from his window, that sinking feeling began to grow. He could always feel it when Kligore was up to something especially rotten. It usually took some awesome investigating to see exactly what Kligore was up to. But not everyone in town was on board with Harry's concerns.

Ever since the town officials had voted to commission the Headless Horseman statue for the town green and change all the Hollow's stores to "terror shops," the fortunes of the town had changed. The cash registers were spilling over with coin, but at the same time, a certain darkness had fallen over the town, like the gray mist swirling above Scarlet Letter Lake.

The Chamber of Commerce's motto for the town, *Sleepy Hollow, Where Every Day is Halloween Night*, seemed to have come true in the daily life of the little New England community.

Not even Christmas was a normal Christmas in Sleepy Hollow, as the store windows featured bad Santas lugging sacks of creepy, demented toys. It was no better at Easter when the scary, fanged Easter Bunny, inside the storefront windows, carried eggs dyed in Kligore's exclusive colors—Blood Red Killer and Dragon Tail Green.

As Harry watched from his window, he knew that somewhere Kligore was indeed hatching another devious plot. But all Harry could do was wait and see what evil would rise from Folly Farm this time around.

4

∞

"All good fun!" Kligore shouted as he sat at the dinner table with his two sons, Titus and Marcus, and his daughter, Clarice. "The spoofing of these holidays is to support our *Spooky Town* brand. We're having fun with them. We're not being serious!"

"Bravo! Dad," Clarice said. "I love all the stuff we make."

"Me too," Marcus said, although he was also busy sloppily chomping on a leg of lamb. "Love it, man."

Titus looked at his father as the chugging, chopping racket from the factory seeped into the mansion's formal dining room. "Why can't we have some peace and quiet around here? Why can't we have a house like Harry Moon's house, just for once?"

Kligore choked on his oysters at the mention of Harry Moon. Clarice spat her mashed potatoes across the room.

"Harry Moon's house! You dare mention that name at the dinner table?" Kligore yelled.

"Yes," Titus said. "I like their house."

Kligore grunted loudly and nudged Clarice. "Hear that, my pretty? Titus likes the Moon house."

"He's got it all wrong, Dad," Clarice said.

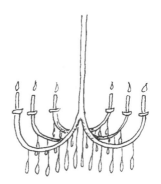

"And so, just what is this Harry Moon's house like, if I might be so bold?" asked the mayor, with a bit of a snarl in his voice.

"Oh, it's great, Pops, if you wanna sit around and pick your nose and watch paint dry," Marcus said once he finished chewing.

"It is not!" Titus said, raising his voice. "You would know if you ever stepped inside!"

Titus's older brother shot back. "I have been as far as I ever want to go into that shack. I went there once trick-or-treating when I was still doing that kinda thing. They didn't even have any mechanical ghosts or slippery snakes at the front door! Really bad, Dad." Marcus grabbed another hunk of lamb. "And their candy was the worst. I mean the worst. It was like healthy stuff—geeze, what a family of goofs."

"I can tell you that home is alive! And it's not boring. It's nice. " Titus pushed his plate away from him.

"So what are you saying? The Kligore home is not alive?" Kligore asked. "Is that what you're saying?"

"It's not the same, Dad."

"Perhaps you'd like to enlighten us," Clarice said.

"Well, like in their dining room. I mean they have these words stenciled on the wall. I kinda like them—joy, love, kindness—you sort of calm down just walking into the room."

Kligore shivered. "WORDS? Gross me out. Why those words are the complete opposite of everything the We Drive by Night Company stands for. How dare you mention them in this home!" Kligore stood up and covered his ears, his eyes flashing.

Titus downed his milk. "Words are powerful, Dad. They can change your mood. I think they can change our personalities. I swear, Dad, there is something going on in that house we don't have here. It's kinda, I don't know, peaceful."

"PEACEFUL!" the mayor shouted. "Who wants that terrible peace?" Kligore slammed his thick fist on the table making his oysters jump off the plate. He slammed so hard that two of the oysters stuck to the ceiling above his head. "Here at the Kligore Mansion, it's all about life! Life should be daring, active, wild. Look around! Our Folly Farm is nothing but life! Sleep when you're dead, Titus. Here, we live!"

"Give me a break," Titus muttered under his breath. "What a load of..."

"Don't say it, man," Marcus said. "Just close your pie hole."

But just as Titus was about to finish his sentence the oysters slipped from the ceiling and landed with a SPLAT! on Kligore's head.

Titus laughed. Kligore stood and with one fell swoop cleared the table with his hand, the empty dishes clattering to the floor.

As half the food from the table fell on the floor, the hounds of Folly Farm—Oink, Trickster, and Nightshade, clawed their way across the slippery floor, fighting one another for the scraps. Oink was the most aggressive, diving into the middle of the feast. Oink was also the most disgusting of all the Kligore creatures.

"Just so you know, Dad, I'm going over to

that *terrible*, peaceful home later. Harry is helping me with my American lit essay," said Titus, wiping Oink's spittle off his pants leg under the table. "Come on Oink! Give me a break! Geesh!"

"Well, Titus, I absolutely do not approve. You know that," Kligore said. "Before you turn around, Moon and his geek squad will be selling you on their ridiculous *Good Mischief Club*."

10

"It's not a club, Dad. It's a team. It's the Good Mischief *Team*."

"Still sounds like the nerd squad to me," said Clarice, jeering.

"They used to be a club. But now they're a team," Titus said. "Because they all work together."

"If it ain't football, it ain't a team," Marcus said.

But then, Kligore grew quiet and calm. He sat down and smiled. "Soooooo," he said like a snake, "you say Mrs. Moon has words on her walls, huh?"

"Yeah," said Titus. "Harry said they were originally stenciled by his great-aunt. But he said his mom repaints them sometimes."

"Stenciling is a wonderful New England tradition," Kligore said. "You've seen our stenciling over the barn doors, right?"

"Yeah," Titus said. "But those words—"

11

Kligore slammed his hand on the table again. "There is nothing wrong with our words. They are words to live by!"

"Yeah," Clarice said. "Our words can beat Moon words any day. Our words are stronger—deceit, envy—"

"Right, my pretty," Kligore said. "Now why don't you just run along and play with one of your Headless Horseman dolls. I want to speak with Titus."

"Okay, Daddy," Clarice said.

Kligore smiled at Titus. "Listen, son, if you're going over there to the Moon house, why don't you pick up one of the new Sleepy Hollow boards at the factory? I am very proud of the stenciling in that game. Let Mrs. Moon know that the font is called Old Salem Woodburn."

"Why?" Titus asked.

12

"She may want to purchase one of our stenciling kits. Old Salem Woodburn is exclusive to the We Drive By Night Company. Those stencil artists love their fonts! Oink will show you where they are. Show him, Oink, will you?"

"I would be delighted to, Master," said the ugly hound, his mouth dripping with oysters and lamb.

Oink bounded over to Titus. The nauseating creature tugged on Titus's jeans with his oily mouth. "You heard your father. Let's get going."

"All right, all right." Titus followed Oink out of the room. They walked down the long, marble corridor where Titus and Marcus raced go-carts in better days. In the days before Sleepy Hollow became Spooky Town.

At the end of the hall, Titus snagged his "THINK DARK" backpack from a hook on the wall.

"Why does he get to go to Harry Moon's when I don't get to go to Larry Barry's house after the games?" Marcus whined.

"Never you mind," said the mayor. "We have to pay more attention to what is happening inside that Moon House. 'Words like peace are powerful'—what the heck? I can't believe any son of mine would ever say such a thing!"

"I dunno." Marcus shrugged. "He's your messed up kid. You really blew it with him."

Kligore looked through the dining room window. He could see Titus and Oink making their way to the factory. "He's more like your mother."

"What?" Marcus said. "I couldn't hear you."

"I said we'll see what words are more powerful. I like the sound of words like confusion and dissension and evil much better, don't you?" Mayor Kligore asked.

14

"I like the word 'chaos' even better!" replied Marcus with a laugh.

Kligore looked down the stretch of table to Marcus and roared with approval. "Now, those are the words of a son of whom I can be proud!"

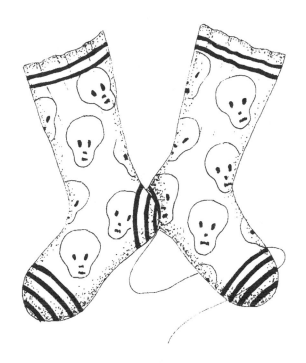

CHILLIE WILLIES' FACTORY

Harry had decided to take a walk even though he was expecting Titus. It was a cool evening. There was a slight breeze which carried the scent of burning leaves. He had walked to the hill overlooking the town. From there he always had a clearer view of Folly Farm and the factory.

The sounds had grown louder and the smoke thicker.

"What are they up to?" he wondered, watching the smoke curl up into the night sky.

Harry looked at his watch. The face glowed with a soft green. "Maybe Titus will have some info."

16

✦

"I want a flawless one, do you hear me? A flawless one!" growled Oink to Chizzie Chowblow, the factory foreman. "Make sure the font is gloss, not matte, and I want it now!"

Titus just stood there in the middle of the warehouse. He never liked to visit the factory. It was gloomy and dark, just like the dolls and toys and games which were manufactured there. As Chizzie hurried, Titus watched as the bodies of the most popular selling toy in Sleepy Hollow rolled down the machine belt—the Headless Horseman Plush Toy.

17

As Titus watched the activity, he felt strange inside. It was like two parts of him battled. There was something about the way his dad ran the business that made him restless. Yes, he had been raised a Kligore and to understand life was always about the buck. It's just that the mayor never stopped. Everything he did was focused on accumulating an even bigger fortune. Like the mayor, the We Drive By Night Company never stopped either, ensuring that *Every Day Is Halloween Night* was true in every nick and corner of Sleepy Hollow. Sometimes, he wondered what it was all about.

His brow sweating, Chizzie Chowblow returned with the Sleepy Hollow Halloween Board. The box was printed in the colors of the village—orange and black—and was covered in dragon-green cellophane. With reverence, Chizzie handed it to Titus as if it were the Holy Grail.

"Did you check it, Chowblow?" Oink grunted.

"I did. I opened it and reinspected it. It's flawless, just as you requested, Master. I then shrink-wrapped it to ensure a perfect package," said Chizzie.

"Attaboy," the dog replied.

Feeling bad that foreman Chizzie Chowblow was being treated like a dog by a dog, Titus nodded and said in an encouraging tone, "It looks really nice, Mr. Chowblow. I am sure that Mrs. Moon will really appreciate the extra care."

Oink growled. "You are such a wussy pants sometimes, Titus. Man up."

Oink led Titus out of the factory and walked with him to the end of Folly Farm's gated grounds. With his backpack over his shoulders and the new game under his arm, Titus passed through the electronic gate of the guard station.

Oink stood at the open gate and barked, "You know what to do?"

"What to do?" Titus said. "I'm going to the Moons to work on my essay."

"The board, Titus. You'll give that board to

19

Mrs. Moon?"

"Of course, I will. Stop treating me like I'm a dumb kid."

"I get concerned about you, boy." The hound growled. "Sometimes you get distracted like you're not even here."

"Oh, I am here all right. You don't have to worry about me," Titus said.

As the lights of the Folly Farm gate dimmed behind him, Titus Kligore walked toward Nightingale Lane. He hoped tonight he would find some of the peace the Moons seemed to have.

SARAH GOOD

Harry rushed to the door when he heard the bell ring. "It's for me."

He pulled open the door and saw Titus standing there with the game tucked under his arm.

"Hey, Kligore," Harry said.

"Hey, Magic," Titus replied.

Harry followed Titus into the living room.

"Oh, hello Titus," Harry's mom said. "I'm glad you could come over. I always enjoy it when you are here."

Titus nodded.

22

"I baked a pie for you guys to snack on," Mom said.

"Pumpkin?" Titus asked.

"Yep," Harry said. "Mom knows it's your favorite."

"Sounds real good, Mrs. Moon," Titus said, smiling. "I think you are the only one who knows my favorite pie. And oh, this is for you. Dad said you might like it."

"How sweet," Mom said. "What is it?"

"It's one of our new games, called The Sleepy Hollow Halloween Board."

She glared at the game through the dragon-green shrink wrap. "Oh, it's a magic board of some kind. How...er...nice. Well, tell your father thank you very much."

"I will," said Titus, shaking his head. "You know my dad. He's a little nuts with all this

But the fruit of the Spirit is love

23

stuff. Always looking for an angle. By making things like this right here in Sleepy Hollow, he doesn't have to share all the profits with the toy companies."

"Of course," Mary said as she looked at the box cover. "Yes, look here—'Be the first in your neighborhood to talk with Sleepy Hollow's Headless Horseman.' Hmm."

Titus flushed with embarrassment. "Mostly, he really wanted you to see the font. Open it, Mrs. Moon."

"Of course," Mary said as she pulled the shrink wrap from the box and opened it. She pulled the wooden board from the box and a little pumpkin-shaped piece of wood on small felt-padded pillars, which acted like a cursor for the board, fell out.

"Oh yes, I know this font—the Old Salem Woodburn. Is that what it is called? It is famous. Leave it to your dad to find it. See the way that S has a line through it? That is how the first woman accused of being a witch, Sarah Good, signed her name. The town used her name with the strange S as the plaque on the gallows before they hung her. They burned Sarah's name into the wood. That's how they arrived at the name of the Old Salem Woodburn font."

"That is pretty creepy," said Titus.

"Look how your father used it in the woodwork here. He used the same S in Sleepy. Leave it to your dad to tie the other famous scary town into a toy from Sleepy Hollow. He's such a branding genius," Mom said.

"And they call me a geek. You guys are font nerds," said Harry.

Harry's mom laughed. "I guess so."

"Come on, Titus. We can work in the dining room," Harry said.

Harry had his American literature book and notebooks sprawled on the dining table.

"Thanks, Moon," Titus said. "I mean for

25

the help. Edgar Allen Poe is kinda hard to understand."

"Sure," Harry said. "Let's get started. Mom will bring the pie soon."

"Cool," Titus said. "I didn't eat much dinner."

Harry opened his text to the poem they had to write an essay about.

26   "Here it is," Harry said. "Have you at least read the whole poem?"

Titus shook his head as he looked around the room. "Nah, but I am reading your wall."

"What, you mean the stencils?"

"Yeah," Titus said.

That was when Mom came in carrying two servings of pumpkin pie with whipped cream.

"They are the pillars that the Moon home is built on," Mom said. "Love, joy, peace, well, you can read them for yourself."

"I know," Titus said. "I have seen them before. I think that's why Dad gave you that game. He said you would appreciate the font we used on the board after I told him how great your stenciling was."

"Thank you, Titus," Mom said.

Harry felt his eyes roll. Why was Titus buttering his mother up like this?

27

"That's the Little Women font up there on the wall," Mom said. "It was the font used by the printer for Little Women. It is said that Louisa May Alcott helped design it."

"Did you know that Steve Jobs' favorite font was Helvetica?" Titus asked.

"I did not know that," answered Mary. "Impressive."

"Not really. I just know about Steve Jobs liking fonts, that's all."

She set the plates on the table and then pulled two forks from her apron pocket. "You boys enjoy."

"Safe," Titus muttered to himself taking a bite of pie.

"What?" Harry said.

"Something about this room in this house makes me feel safe," Titus said.

"Me too," Harry said. "Safer than that stupid board you brought us."

Titus swallowed. "What are you talking about Moon? There ain't nothing wrong with that Halloween Board. It's just a game.

"More like a door into hell," Harry said.

And that was when Harry's dad walked into the dining room. He was wiping his hands on a dish towel. "Hey guys, what's up in our peaceful castle?" he asked. "Hi, Titus. Sorry, I'm a greasy mess. I was just working on the car."

"Oh, Titus has just brought hell's door into our castle," said Harry as he took another bite of pie.

"Er...I didn't plan on that, Mr. Moon, really. My dad wanted you and Mrs. Moon to see the font."

Dad grabbed the box from the breakfront. "Oh, huh. Interesting." He opened the box, pulled out the board, and the pumpkin-shaped piece fell out onto the floor.

29

Just seeing the board gave Harry the creeps. "Come on, Dad put that tool of hell back in its casket"

30

TROUBLE

"You have to keep the essay in one tense or the other," Harry said. "You have to decide."

Titus and Harry both had their laptops cracked opened, and Harry was reviewing Titus's essay on Edger Allan Poe on his screen. "You have to choose and just stay with it. Mrs. Hershey is going to pull the paper down a whole grade if you don't keep to one tense."

"This whole thing is makin' me tense," Titus said.

"Good one, but seriously you have to concentrate."

"Okey dokey," said Titus.

Harry and Titus continued working for another hour before Titus's cell buzzed. He glanced at the screen. "It's my father. Probably wants me to get home."

"Okay," Harry said.

"Thanks, Magic. I owe you. I guess we could have skyped, but I kinda like coming over here sometimes. It's a nice escape from my world," Titus said. "I could use a little peace."

"Let's not overdo the peace thing," Harry said. "Don't you remember my little sister? The queen of chaos? I'm surprised she's left us alone this long."

"It's just that even when there's chaos here, it simmers down pretty fast. At Folly Farm, nothing simmers down. It always seems like it's going to blow."

Harry Moon was always careful with Titus. While Harry suspected Mayor Maximus Kligore was a dark lord with ties to evil, he could not prove it. Without knowing the full truth, Harry never wanted to impart his suspicions to Titus. He knew how unhappy Titus was with his home life.

33

"Titus, you know my folks like you, though I have no idea why, but you are always welcome over at the Moon Palace."

"Thanks, Harry."

As Titus picked up his "THINK DARK" backpack, Honey slipped into the dining room and said, "Boo, boys!"

"What'd I tell ya?" Harry said. "The queen of chaos."

34

"Soooo, Brother, did you two numskulls get your homework done? Mine's been finished for hours."

"Awww, you're just a kid," Titus said. "With kiddie homework."

"Yeah," Harry said. "We have the hard work to do."

Titus slung his backpack over his shoulder.

"Thanks again, Moon."

"Sure, I'll walk you to the door."

"By the way, Titus," Honey said, smiling sweetly. "If you ever have trouble with spelling come see me. Harry couldn't spell if his life depended on it."

Titus laughed. "Yeah, okay, I'll remember that."

"Stop your bragging, queen of the spelling bee, and go find a flower!" Harry said as he went marching toward her. Honey ran out of the room

"So much for peace," Harry said.

"Aww, it's still better than my house. Clarice is a total pain, worse than Honey. She swapped out the shampoo in my bathroom with mayonnaise the other day."

Harry cracked up. "Seriously? Now that's funny."

Titus laughed along with him. "Yeah, it was a pretty genius prank. But it took me forever to get the smell out of my hair. The guys at lunch kept saying they were having cravings for BLTs."

Harry watched until Titus had disappeared into the dark. He let out a sigh. It must be pretty tough growing up on Folly Farm.

It was a little on the late side when Titus left. Harry's mom and dad had already gone to bed. But Harry wanted another slice of pie before he hit the sack. He was in the kitchen spraying whipped cream on a slice when he heard a noise in the dining room.

"Honey," he said, "what are you doing in here? You should be in bed."

"I wanted to get a closer look at the Sleepy Hollow Halloween Board."

"You mean the portal to hell. I'd stay away."

"That's ridiculous. It's just a game."

Honey opened the breakfront and grabbed the game. She opened the orange and black box. "Oh, it's beautiful," she said. "The artwork is gorgeous. Mom was right."

"Honey, don't you know what it's for?"

"It predicts the future or something." Honey set the board on the table and then placed the pumpkin-shaped planchette on top.

"No," Harry said. "It's for contacting the dark side in Sleepy Hollow."

"Oh, well it's not for real anyways, right?" Honey ran her fingers over the board.

"Let's just put it away," replied Harry.

"Yeah," Honey said, pulling her hand away from the board. "I do feel a little creepy." She swallowed and shivered.

"Who knows what evil has been carried

into this house with that game," Harry grimaced. "Think maybe we should go to bed."

"Okay," Honey said.

That night Harry had trouble sleeping. He kept thinking about the mayor's gift and wondering why he *really* wanted the Moon family to have it. It just didn't smell right. In fact, it smelled downright terrible.

He looked at his clock. 11:59.

Something felt funny in the air. "What is going on?" Harry said to the darkness. And in that second his great-aunt's grandfather clock struck midnight. *GONG. GONG.*

"What the heck?" Harry sat up. "That clock's been broken for years."

As Harry lay back in his bed counting the chimes, the whole house seemed to shudder with each strike. The Edgar Allan Poe poem,

"The Bells," that he and Titus had been studying echoed in his brain.

> *Oh, the bells, bells, bells!*
> *What a tale their terror tells...*
> *How they clang, and clash, and roar!*
> *What a horror they outpour...*
> *By the sinking or the swelling in the*
>   *anger of the bells—*
> *Of the bells—*
> *Of the bells, bells, bells, bells...*
> *In the clamor and the clangor of the*
>   *bells!*

39

Harry sat up again. The bedroom's dark air shimmered with hidden life.

The closet door creaked, swelling ever so slightly. It was as if a monster, trapped inside the closet, was pushing again and again at the wooden door to break it down. Harry sucked in a deep breath. He shivered.

He felt movement beneath him and sensed life thumping below his bed. He could hear nothing, but he sensed the darkness swirling beneath him. Still, there was only the silence. Silence and the dark. The only noises were verses of poetry in his brain.

> By the sinking or the swelling in the anger
>   of the bells—
> Of the bells—
> Of the bells, bells, bells, bells...
> In the clamor and the clangor of the bells!

Even though he was scared, Harry kept telling himself that he really had nothing to fear. Even though he wasn't visible at the moment, Rabbit was near.

He slowly leaned out over the side of the bed. He gasped as what he was seeing. "That can't be, can't be," he whispered to himself. It wasn't a monster or even a ghost. Harry saw waves of his own socks pushing out from beneath the edge of the bed and then ebbing back like tide water pulled by moonlight.

"My socks?" Harry said. "Now, I must be dreaming."

With a loud groan, the closet door buckled. Harry saw the brass knob turn counterclockwise. The door flew open with a start. A leg stepped out. Just a leg. No body, no head, no arms. Just a leg. The calf was thin and crooked, like a gnarled tree root, and it wore a black-and-orange striped knee-high sock. It was almost laughable, but not. Harry wanted to scream. A second leg, also in orange-and-black stripes emerged from the closet.

41

Together, the weird, disembodied legs stepped to the middle of Harry's bedroom floor. With Edgar Allan Poe's words burned in his head, Harry watched as the pair of legs in stockings danced a jig.

In the silence of the night,
How we shiver with affright...
For every sound that floats,
From the rust within their throats...
Of the bells—
Of the bells, bells, bells, bells,
Bells, bells, bells—
In the clamor and the clangor of the bells!

The dance was full of fury even though there were only two legs dancing, dancing a dance that felt most macabre. The strange legs rocked to the words which ran sing-song in his head. Harry pulled the sheet and blanket over his eyes.

"This isn't happening, Moon. This is not happening. You're dreaming."

Harry closed his eyes, trying to block the image of the legs from his mind. Tossing and turning, he attempted to shake the bell song from his thoughts.

Harry felt pressure at the corner of his bed; a weight on his feet. The pressure came in fits like the dark, rolling tide underneath the bed frame. Harry pulled the blanket off his eyes. He looked at the foot of the bed. The orange-and-black striped stockings still danced.

"Scram! Get out of my room!" Harry ordered.

But the legs only danced harder. Harry reached out to swipe them away, but his hands swiped right through the legs.

"Something has broken through the darkness," Harry said. "Something evil."

For a second or two, the legs disappeared. Harry lay back down with the covers pulled tightly over his head. Yet the legs came back and danced on his bed, on his back, and on his head.

"Get off of me," he said. "Go back to where you came from! Go back to the pit of hell!"

43

Harry told them three times to go away and finally, at long last there was silence. The music was gone. His head dripped with perspiration. The room was finally quiet.

44

STRIPED SOCKS AND SCHOOL SPIRIT

When morning finally came, Harry jumped out of bed. The events of last night remained fresh in his mind.

"That just had to have been a dream," he said.

His closet door was wide open. With the morning light slanting through the window, the closet no longer held the dark abyss of night. Harry picked through his clothes on the hangers and other things in the closet. "Normal. Normal. All normal."

But as he took a step forward, he noticed something soft under his toes. It was the orange-and-black striped socks that danced around his room. He picked up the stockings

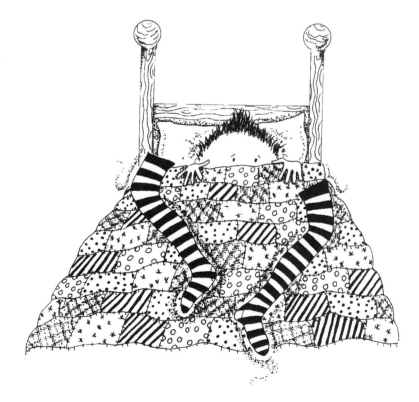

with one hand, holding them between his thumb and index finger as if it were a dead squirrel or a stinky fish.

"Ugh, I must have been dreaming. These are Honey's socks. How did they get in here?" He marched across the hall and knocked on Honey's door, not caring if he woke her or not. No answer. He knocked again. "Honey. Hey, Honey," he called through the door, "open up. It's me."

"Come in," his sister called in a groggy voice.

Harry pushed open the door. Honey was still in her bed, face down. "What do you want?" she whispered into her pillow. "What time is it?"

"Are these yours?" Harry asked, holding up the striped socks.

Honey opened one eye. "*Hey*, drop those right there. Those are mine. What are you doing with my socks?"

"Your socks were in my room. I have no clue how they got there." He held the two socks out to her.

"What were you doing with them?" Honey sat up and glared at Harry. "Those are spirit socks! All the girls in my class wear them on Fridays to show our school loyalty. I have not been able to find them. You better not be using my stuff for your stupid magic tricks. I'm telling Mom."

"Don't worry. I'm not touching your stuff, especially your smelly socks. Gimme a break." Harry said.

"Well, leave my stuff alone," Honey said. "School spirit is important. And how do I really know you didn't come in here and steal them? You're probably doing something lame with them."

"I wouldn't get caught dead in your room. And I don't use crummy props like your stinky socks. Maybe Mom got them mixed up in the laundry, did you ever think of that?"

Honey shook her head. "I seriously doubt Mom could get my spirit socks mixed up with your ugly, white tube socks."

"Yeah, right." Harry went back to his room and got ready for school. He tried to push the dancing socks from his mind by telling himself it was just a dream. But still, there was just something too vivid about it. A strange vibe overtook his room. Getting away to school this morning might be the best thing.

49

As Harry ate his blueberries and oatmeal at the dining room table, Mom called from the kitchen. "Harry, have you seen my bag?"

"It's on the hall table," he said.

"Thanks, sweetheart. Would you like a ride to school?"

Harry swallowed another bite of oatmeal. "It's okay, I have time to walk, but thanks," Harry said.

Mary Moon came over to Harry and kissed

him on the top of his head. "Have a good day, sweetie. Will you help get Honey out the door too? She's running late again."

"Speaking of Honey, Mom, you seem to be mixing up Honey's clothes with mine," Harry said.

"I did? How?"

"I found her spirit socks on my bedroom floor this morning. Maybe you dropped them?"

Mom looked sternly into Harry's eyes. "First of all, Harry, what does it really matter if I did? You are right across the hall from her room. And secondly, you brought the last load of laundry to your room. Remember?"

Harry swallowed. Hard. "Uhm, right, Mom. It was just that...I was wondering how they got there. That's all."

"Okay, I gotta run. Mrs. Wilcox is with Harvest."

Honey sashayed into the room and dropped her turtle backpack on the floor. "Well, if it isn't the sock thief," she said.

"Yeah, yeah," said Harry. "You got me. Gonna arrest me?"

"If only I could."

Honey opened the breakfront.

"What are you doing?" Harry asked.

51

"I was just gonna check out that game Titus brought over again."

"No," Harry said. "Leave it alone. It's weird. And besides you have to go to school. Now."

"Awww, c'mon, Harry. I just want to look."

She pulled the game from the cabinet and set it on the table. "It is pretty. Very inviting. It almost calls you to play with it, doesn't it?"

Harry stood and grabbed the game

away from Honey. "No time for this."

"All right, all right, sock thief. Geeze. It's a game. I don't really believe that mumbo jumbo."

"Good," Harry said. "We should leave."

"Okay, Brother, and I cannot wait to wear my spirit socks on Friday."

"Now that I found them," Harry said.

"Now that you gave them back."

Harry and Honey hurried out of the house. They headed down the walk toward school.

"I still don't understand how your socks got in my room," Harry said. "It's weird."

Honey stopped walking. "We do live in Sleepy Hollow, Harry. Everything here is a little weird."

Harry gave his sister a little shoulder punch. "You're right. But hey, did you ever wonder why socks get lost so much?"

Honey shrugged. "Not really, I think it's just one of life's big mysteries, like true love."

"I guess so," Harry said. But still, he had a gnawing feeling in the pit of his stomach that something was not quite right. There was definitely something afoot in Sleepy Hollow.

"And I'm gonna figure it out," Harry said.

"What?" Honey said.

"Nothing, I'll see you later."

Harry headed off to school in the opposite direction of his sister. When he got to the town green, he stopped at the Headless Horseman statue. "Hey, Goofy," he called up to the statue's head. "Did you put those socks in my room?"

"Of course not, Harry," came a voice from behind the statue.

53

"What? Wait a second, who's there?"

A short, pudgy hound made himself visible. "It's me, Moon."

"Oink! You crumb, what do you want?"

"I was just wondering how your family was enjoying the new Sleepy Hollow Halloween Board."

"We aren't enjoying it," Harry said.

"Ohhhhh welllllll, you should really give it a spin. Did your mother at least enjoy that special font?"

"Yes, but so what? Why would she care about a stupid, old-timey font? And who cares about Sarah Good?"

"Oh, so she *did* recognize it," Oink said. "Mayor Kligore will be most pleased. He couldn't get anything out of that crazy kid, Titus." Then Oink shoved a mangy paw over his snout. "Oh dear," he mumbled. "I might have said too much. Silly me." And with a glint in his eye, Oink scampered off across the green like he was any old dog.

"Said too much? Now I know something is up," Harry said, watching Oink disappear around the back of City Hall.

55

56

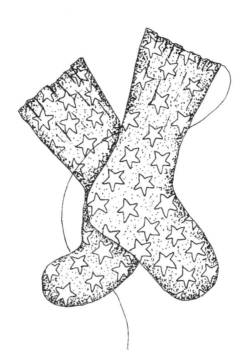

Missing Sock Theory

B y the time lunchtime rolled around,
Harry was feeling exhausted. It had
been a long night, and his morning
was so filled with many questions and few
answers that he was drained by the time
lunchtime rolled around. And he had the
early lunch.

Harry sat at his usual table with Declan,
Hao, and Bailey.

"So, what's new, boys?" Declan asked.

Hao swallowed a bit of PB&J. "Nothing with me. Same old boring stuff."

"Yeah, me too," Bailey said. "We could use some excitement around here."

Harry was staring into his pudding cup.

"What about you, Moon?" Bailey said. "How's tricks?"

Harry looked up. "Nothing," he said.

"What?" Declan said.

"Nothing is new with me," Harry said. "At least, I don't think so." He looked at his friends who were staring at him like he had tomatoes growing off the top of his head. "I was just wondering something, though. Where do all the socks go?"

"Yep, it's finally happened. He's lost his mind," Hao said.

"No, really," Harry said. "I mean like around the house. You know when you put six socks into the dryer but only five come out. Where did the other sock go?"

"Oh, I gotcha," Declan said. "It's called sock theory. There are actually several different theories about this strange phenomenon."

"Yeah," Hao said. "It is weird. And I think it happens in every house. We lose socks all the time."

"Us too," Bailey said. "So really, where do they go?"

"Explain that sock theory stuff," said Hao.

"There are basically three theories," Declan said holding up three fingers. "The first is the practical one. It involves the washer or the dryer. The sock falls between the outer and inner drum of the washer or in that same space in the dryer. Lost forever. Gone."

"Yeah, well I tried that first theory, bro,"

Hao replied. "I took the washer and the dryer apart with a Phillips screwdriver, and there were no socks, only a big repair bill from Sears and three weeks grounded." He shoved a chicken nugget into his mouth. "Three weeks."

"Well, that leads us to the second theory. The Parallel Universe Theory," Declan said. He took a swig of milk. "Between the universe we know and the unknown universe we fear, there are dryers. When dryers are hot and spinning fast, the portal between the two worlds opens. It's called dimension slippage. Socks and underwear are bound to get sucked up when the portal is opened, wouldn't you think?"

"That's the one I am betting on," said Bailey, shaking his head. "That's the one I believe fits."

Harry was still not satisfied. Nothing seemed to make sense to him. And he hadn't even told the guys about the dancing socks yet. To be honest, Harry wasn't so sure he should tell them. But they were the Good Mischief Team, and they had to know if something dark was happening.

"The third theory involves dark matter, only applicable to foot-worn garments not to underwear. Because of the constant pressure the foot places on the front area of the sock, the sock develops an unusually low density at the toe." He paused for a second and chewed. "When the hyper-heat of the dryer meets the low density of the sock toe, dark matter forms—a hole, as it were, in the space-time continuum."

"Where do you come up with this stuff?" Hao asked.

Harry looked at the cafeteria clock. Lunch was almost over. So he took a deep breath and said. "Okay, so there are theories about socks getting lost. But what about socks that come ALIVE!"

Bailey spat apple juice across the table. "Hah. You are one goofy, wing nut magician, Moon."

"Hold on, hold on," Hao said. "Let's hear what Houdini has to say."

"Listen," Harry said. "I thought you guys might not believe me but here's what happened."

The guys could not take their eyes off Harry as he told them all about his night with the dancing socks.

"And when I woke up this morning," Harry said, "I found my sister's spirit socks on my floor."

"Spirit socks?" Declan said. "You mean, woooooooo, eerie spirit, right?"

"Not really," Harry said. "I mean my sister's orange-and-black school socks. All the girls wear them on Fridays. Honey hasn't been able to find them."

63

"Until last night," Hao said. "When they came dancing out of your closet."

"Right," Harry replied. "I know it sounds impossible but—"

"Wait a minute, wait a minute!" Declan said. "We have a problem. I don't know everything about dark matter or fifth dimensions, but it sounds like the Moon household has a case of spooky socks."

Harry's heart raced. "Spooky socks?"

"Do you not get the timing? When did those socks come into your room?" asked Bailey.

"Last night," Harry replied. "Around midnight."

"Oooooooo, the witching hour," Hao said.

Harry swallowed. "Yeah, I know."

"And when did the Sleepy Hollow Halloween Board show up?"

"Yesterday," said Harry.

"Check it out. Mayor Kligore sends his dough-head son, Titus, over with the board," Bailey said.

"Don't call him a dough-head, Bailey. He's a guy like the rest of us," said Harry. "And he was really kind of nice."

"Yeah. A regular guy whose dad just happens to be the Mayor from Hell. Of course, no connection or anything."

"We don't know anything *definitive* about Titus," Harry said.

"But we have our suspicions, right, Harry, especially about the evil spell that his dad may have placed on Sleepy Hollow to get everyone jazzed about making money?" Bailey asked.

"Yes, we have our suspicions," Harry said. "But what is Kligore up to? With the socks, I mean."

65

"As far as I can see, there's just one thing to do in this case of spooky socks," said Hao as he shoved his trash into a lunch bag.

"What's that?" Harry asked.

"The Vampire Vanquishing Kit," Hao said.

"But they're not vampires," Harry said. "They're socks."

Hao and the others picked up their trays and headed for the trash bins. "Whatever made those socks dance comes from the same evil place that allows vampires to live for centuries," Hao said.

"You mean the pit of Hell," Harry said. "I thought so."

"Yep," Hao said. "That evil sock stuff came in attached to that Halloween Board."

"But," said Harry as he dropped his trash in the can, "I don't get it. I've been helping out Titus. He wouldn't do anything like this to me or my family!"

"Titus didn't do anything. He was a tool, man. That's all," Declan replied. "He was just getting used by his old man."

"That creep," Hao said. "Kligore is such a jerk."

"He is," Bailey said. "And the Good Mischief Team is gonna stop him."

"Right," Harry said. "We have to."

Declan gave Harry a push down the hall. "We'll unravel this sock mystery."

Harry pushed him back. "You are so weird."

67

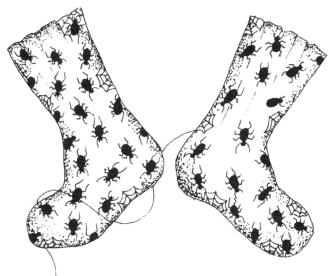

FRIENDLY CONFUSION

Harry was on his way to his seventh period physics class when he spotted Titus Kligore in the school hallway. It was hard to miss Titus as he was the tallest student in eighth grade. Titus stood six feet four inches tall—the same height as his dad, the mayor, and his brother, Marcus.

Harry, the shortest kid in eighth grade, caught the eye of the giant, giving him the nod to step free of the changeover jam. Titus walked to the left side of the hallway, and Harry made his way through the crowd of students and joined him.

"What's up?" Titus said.

"I have to ask you a question. Promise me you won't lie," said Harry.

"I'll try."

"No, you gotta do the Yoda thing. 'No try, Titus, only do.'"

"Yes, Obi-Wan." Titus smiled.

"No, I was Yoda," Harry said. He leaned against a locker.

"Then who am I?"

"Technically, you would be Luke, 'cause Yoda said that to Luke."

"Oh right," Titus said.

"Look, that doesn't matter; you just got to be straight with me. About that Halloween Board, what do you know about it?"

Titus scratched his head. "It's a stupid moneymaker toy for my dad's company."

"And anything else?"

"No, just what your mom told me about the font and Sarah Good. How she was a witch and all."

71

Harry did his best to look into Titus's eyes. Maybe he really didn't have a clue about what his father was doing.

"Just tell me why you brought that thing over to my house."

"My dad," said Titus. "He wanted your mom to have it 'cause she knows fonts, that's all."

"And do you do everything your dad tells

you to do?"

"Pretty much. I mean, Harry, I am not as stupid as your friends think I am."

"They don't think you are stupid."

"Yes, they do. But I can think on my own. Listen, Moon, my dad is powerful, rich, and really stubborn. My mom ran out on us. What am I supposed to do? My older brother is a suck up. My father is all I have." Titus looked away from Harry. Then he took a deep breath and said, "So what? Did I do anything wrong by bringing that game over? Did something happen?"

Harry had to think a moment. Did he really want to tell Titus about the socks?

"Yeah," Harry said. "At least, I think it has something to do with the board."

"So tell me. What happened?"

That was when Mr. Crenshaw walked past them. "Get a move on, boys," he said. "You're late for class."

"Okay," Harry said. "On our way."

"What happened, Moon?" Titus asked. It seemed the bullying part of Titus was coming out again.

"Last night, Honey's socks came out of my closet and danced all over my room."

Titus threw his head back and laughed. "Wozie. Harry, you're probably one of the greatest magicians in the world, if not the greatest." Titus leaned down and took Harry's right shoulder and shook it with affection. "Don't you think those dancing socks had more to do with you and your awesome magic and less to do with that stupid moneymaking board? Heck, those spooky socks were probably auditioning for your next magic show."

Harry snorted air out of his nose. Titus obviously didn't have a clue about the socks.

"I guess you're right," Harry said. He just wanted to end the conversation for now. "We better get to class."

"Catch you later?" Titus said with a smile. Harry nodded and was off to his next class.

But still, Harry was confused.

That night, Harry was studying for his physics test when a text came in on his phone from Hao Jones.

"The Vampire Vanquishing Kit is not inconsistent with your beliefs," the text read.

Harry picked up his cell.

He tapped the letters. "How so?"

"Ever seen a vampire kit?" the text read.

"No. Just heard 'bout it."

"It contains everything we need to vanquish the evil dudes."

"Why?"

"The bloodsuckers fear its truth," the text read.

Harry tapped TL and clicked send.

He closed his physics book and climbed into his bed. He was a little concerned about what tonight's witching hour might bring.

"What am I, chopped liver?" the familiar voice asked.

It was Rabbit.

"Rabbit!" Harry said. "Where have you been?"

"You can listen to Titus and Hao, but you don't have time to look me up? I'm not far off, you know. Some might even say that, when I'm around, Heaven has arrived."

Rabbit sat on Harry's desk.

"I'm sorry, Rabbit," Harry said. "I've just had a lot on my mind."

"That's when you find me," Rabbit replied. "You were right when you told your friends that you needed to continue to remind yourself of the power of good. There will always be forces that try to tear you down. You have to continue to look for me. The trick is not to be afraid of the dark. And dancing socks."

"You are so right, Rabbit. You are always right," Harry said.

"I better be. I am Rabbit, after all."

Harry laughed as he put his hands behind his head and stared at the dark ceiling above his bed. "I have missed you, friend," Harry said.

"There's never a reason to miss me, Harry. I am always right beside you."

Harry looked at Rabbit across the bedroom. Moonlight crept through the window blinds, casting a strange shadow across Rabbit's face.

"So, tell me," Rabbit said, "what's on your mind?"

Harry thought about the events of the last few days. He was worried about lots of things—the socks, the Halloween Board—but he was also worried about Titus. Which was weird because Titus was always his nemesis and had pulled some pretty rotten pranks on him. "I'm worried about Titus," Harry said. "I shouldn't be. After all, he's the one who cut my hair off and a bunch of other stuff."

"That was a different time," Rabbit said. "But the both of you have moved on. You have to keep encouraging him. Just like you are doing. I'm proud of you, Harry."

Rabbit hopped to the foot of Harry's bed.

Harry looked across his feet to Rabbit.

"I'm trying," Harry said. "But how can I do that when he lives in a house full of so much evil?"

"Point him in the right direction. We all need that encouragement. Be like Yoda, right? Do not try, do."

"You've been spying on me, again," said Harry.

"How can I be spying if I am right beside you?"

"I guess you're right," Harry said.

Harry closed his eyes. He was feeling sleepy. But he also wanted to keep talking to Rabbit. "Rabbit," he said opening his eyes. "Is there any hope for Titus?"

"Lead by example. Soon, maybe he'll have a Rabbit just like you do."

80

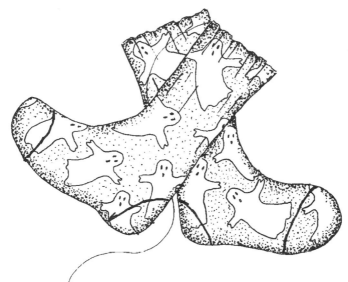

DARK FINGERS

Once again, Harry awoke to the ringing of the bells in the grandfather clock.

One, two, three—the bells struck. *Four, five, six. Seven, eight, nine.* His heart raced. "Not again," he said hoping Rabbit was still sitting on his desk. Or better yet, at the foot of his bed. But he wasn't.

"This whole witching hour thing is just an old, ridiculous legend, an old wives tale," Harry whispered into the dark. Still, he could not keep from counting.

Ten, eleven, twelve.

"I will not let fear sabotage my mind!" he thought, gritting his teeth and pressing the back of his head against the pillow. The pillow on his bed was already damp with sweat.

They are Ghouls:
And their king it is who tolls;
And he rolls, rolls, rolls...
A paean for the bells;
And his merry bosom swells...
And he dances, and he yells...
To the tolling of the bells, bells, bells!

The clock struck the final bell, and that same eerie gloom filled Harry's room. He looked at his closet. The door was shut. Tight. It didn't bulge like it had the night before. No, tonight Harry felt the presence was under his bed. He gripped the sides of his mattress as he forced fear from his brain and body.

82

Like the gloved hands of a jinni, dark fingers rose out of the four corners of Harry's bed. He tried with all his might and all his mind to fight the fear. Then Harry remembered something his father had told him. Courage and bravery can only arrive once they walk past fear. It is not that the brave aren't afraid; they are brave in spite of the fear.

The gloved fingers that rose from the bed were more than two hands. As Harry looked out from the middle of the bed, there were hundreds of cloaked and woolen fingers rising over the rim of the mattress. At first, they looked like fence slats, as if they were trying to imprison Harry. As they surged upward, the slats turned inward like a palm with one hundred fingers scheming to grab the wizard into the dark mystery of its gloomy hand.

83

"What do you want from me?" Harry shouted. He stood up on the bed to escape from the rising fingers, all gloved in socks.

"Where do you come from?" he asked.

"D A R K N E S S," the voice answered.

The voice was low. It lurked in the gloomy atmosphere. Harry looked for the source. But he saw nothing. Not a mouth or a tongue. The voice filled the room.

Harry jumped, grabbing the bedpost, and peered out over the bed frame. He looked down and down and seemed to be falling deeper and deeper until he fell to the floor.

Then he saw it—what appeared to be a mouth of darkness beneath the bed. Strangely,

like mist, the fingers stretched out from the mouth, forming a wooly tongue.

Harry yelled as the tongue of darkness pushed forward.

"Do no evil!" Harry shouted at the moving darkness. "Do no evil!" Harry was expecting an answer. But it didn't come from the mouth of gloom beneath his bed.

It came from behind him. As he turned, he heard the closet speak.

"No, no! That's not it, Harry Moon," came the voice inside the closet.

The closet door crashed open. From the deep abyss of darkness, the orange-and-black striped stockings kicked their way toward him.

"Those are not the words to the spell! No, Harry, that is not it!"

The stocking gamboled forward. The thin calf of the leg with the gnarled thigh kicked

Harry. The toe of the thing hit Harry on the chin. The boy magician careened backward onto the floor.

As he lay on the carpet, the tongue from beneath the bed lashed forward. The orange-and-black striped stockings, disembodied and forceful, pranced toward him, stamping like thunder.

With all his strength, Harry stood and ran to the door. He pulled the knob. But the door would not open. Then with a crash, the door flew open. Harry ran as hard he could, but the other bedrooms were gone, gone from this dark night.

It was not the hallway he knew. It was nothing but an airy wall of gloom. The wall moaned and groaned and creaked from every particle of its miserable essence.

"Darkness," it said. "Darkness. Darkness."

Harry fell into the abyss. His body tumbled and somersaulted deeper and deeper into the dark sleep. He was asleep inside the song of the witching hour and never heard the clock strike one.

AFTERMATH

Harry's mother had to wake him the next morning, which was odd because Harry was always awake on time. At first, she thought he might be sick.

"Are you okay, Harry?" she asked.

Harry rubbed his eyes, sitting up. "Huh, yeah, I think so. Sorry, Mom."

"It's okay," Mom said. "But you better get a move on. You'll be late. I can drive you this morning."

"Thanks, Mom," Harry said.

"No problem," she said, "but why is there a pile of socks on your bed?"

Harry looked and, sure enough, there at the bottom of the bed was a pile of socks. At the top of the heap was a red-and-green hand-knit sock which his great-aunt Debbie had knit for him. It had been missing for a long time.

Mom grabbed the sock from the top of the heap, inspecting it. The sock bore the unmistakable pattern of red wagons and green bicycles.

"Look, Harry," she said happily, "I'm so surprised. I never thought I would see this sock again. They're the Christmas socks that your great-aunt Debbie had knit for you a few years ago. God rest her soul."

Truth be told, Harry was probably even more surprised than his mom was, seeing that red-and-green sock again. "I know," he said.

"Well, get going. I'll meet you in the kitchen."

"Okay, Mom," Harry said. "Be there in five."

"Great," she said as she bent down. She held Honey's orange-and-black socks. "How did these get in here again?"

Harry shrugged. "I don't know, Mom."

"Fine," she said. "Now hurry."

Harry dressed quickly, but there was no time for breakfast. He chose his "DO NO EVIL" t-shirt because he had a feeling he might just need a little more courage today, and the shirt kind of helped him feel stronger. He dashed out the back door and climbed into the front seat of his Mom's minivan. Fortunately, Sleepy Hollow

Middle School was in the same direction as the hospital.

"Honestly, Mom, I don't know how those socks got there," Harry said.

"When you were little, you used to sleepwalk," Mom said as she pulled onto the street. "In the morning, your dad and I would find Chips Ahoy! and Oreo cookies on your bed. Sometimes we would find you asleep in the den. Do you remember?"

"I remember you telling me about it," Harry said.

"Maybe you're sleepwalking again."

Harry looked out the car window. "I don't think so."

Mom turned onto School Lane. "Maybe it's your magic? Could it be that?"

"If it's magic, it's not *my* magic," Harry said as they passed the statue of the school mascot. Harry never liked that huge, black raven.

"I have an idea," Mom said. She stopped the car in the drop-off zone. "Why don't you pop by and see Samson Dupree? He might be able to help you figure things out."

"Maybe," Harry said. "Samson does know a lot about stuff like this."

That afternoon, Harry took his mom's advice even though Declan and Hao wanted him to go to the pizza shop.

"Nah," Harry told them. "I got something else to do."

"More sock stuff?" Declan asked.

"Yeah," Harry replied. "It happened again last night."

"Wow," Hao said. "I sure hope you get this

mystery solved. You look awful."

"Thanks," Harry said. "Thanks a lot."

It was one of those marvelous days. White, fluffy clouds chuffed through a brilliant, blue sky. The sun shone brightly. Even though he was troubled, and his mind was filled with worry, the weather lightened Harry's burden for a while. He thought maybe Samson was already working some of his special magic.

The Sleepy Hollow Magic Shoppe was one of Harry's favorite places. It was here that he first learned many of his special magic skills. Samson was a good friend and a good mentor. Harry trusted Samson with his life and his soul.

Harry always sat on the special bar stool behind the counter, which he considered especially reserved for him. Harry felt special in that chair. In the end, of course, it had less to do with the chair and more to do with the company. Harry was extremely fond of Samson Dupree. While he was eccentric, often wearing capes and crowns and weird bright shoes, Samson was an adult who genuinely seemed interested in Harry. Of course, they shared the same fascination for magic, but it was more than that. Harry always felt that Samson was truly fascinated by life, itself, but most particularly, Harry's life.

"Have a magical life!" Samson always said to him. "There is a reason we are alive! To love and give joy!"

Sometimes, Harry thought that Samson might be some kind of prophet, because of his eccentric forecasts. More often, Harry wondered if Samson might even be his guardian angel because he seemed to know more about Harry than Harry knew. The one thing Harry knew for sure—whether prophet or angel—Samson was always kind.

Harry pushed open the Magic Shoppe door. He loved the sound of the little bell.

Harry told Samson the whole story. From beginning to end. He told him about Titus and the Sleepy Hollow Halloween Board. He told him about the socks and fingers and the darkness that lurked under his bed. He told Samson about falling into a dark abyss and how he struggled to remain calm and muster his courage.

When he had finished, Harry took a deep breath. It felt good to let it all out.

96

"Wowie zowie," Samson said. "That's quite a story."

"But you believe me, right, Samson?" Harry asked.

"Of course I do, Harry. I had a feeling something was going on."

"So what do you make of the voice saying, 'No, Harry, you don't have it right about 'do no evil'?"

Samson looked into Harry's eyes. Most of the time, when people looked that deeply at him, Harry felt nervous. But when Samson did it, he felt comfortable.

"It's known as the *dark twisting*," Samson said.

Harry gasped. "Dark twisting? What does it *mean*?"

Samson set a bowl of cashews and

pistachios onto the counter. "Have a snack, Harry. You look tired."

"Thanks, Samson."

"Darkness tries to trip us up," Samson said. "It mixes lies with truth, and we become confused. Unfortunately, in the confusion, that's when evil really moves in."

Samson thought for a while. Harry liked it when the old magician pondered, stroking his head and scratching his stack of jet-black hair. This thinking usually produced a resulting question that was always pretty good. "Now, how many times have these strange stockings appeared?"

"Twice," said Harry.

"Yes, yes, very good then, the dark twisting is coming. Now that you know it is coming, you'll be ready to chase it down."

"What do you mean?"

"Darkness has started twisting the truth." Samson popped a cashew into his mouth. "It has told you that you are wrong about 'Do No Evil.' Next time around, darkness will tease you with a blend of lies and truth. Most people get confused here, and they start believing what the darkness has to say."

"Can you tell me what darkness is going to say?"

"You'll find out soon enough. Tonight in fact."

99

Harry coughed. A bit of pistachio had gotten caught in his throat. "Tonight? You mean I have to go through it *again?*"

Samson nodded. "Yes, Harry. It will be a lie to confuse you. So be ready for it."

Harry studied Samson's face. It was young yet ancient. "I will be."

Samson stood and straightened some things on the counter. "So Harry, what else is on your mind?"

"Last night, I called out to Rabbit, and he did not come."

Samson rubbed his belly and seemed to suppress a laugh. "Harry, Rabbit will always come."

"But he wasn't there."

100

"Oh, he was there, all right. But darkness is a powerful thing. Just a hunch, but you were blind-folded. The cloth was so thick in its weave, you could not see Rabbit."

"Really?" Harry said. "But I didn't feel a blindfold."

Samson shook his head. "You wouldn't. And that dang Edgar Allan Poe poem was so loud, you could not hear."

"It was," Harry said. "I tried to shut it off, but I couldn't."

"The light never leaves," Samson said. "It does not abandon us. Sometimes darkness seems overwhelming. There are circumstances, perhaps this is one of them, which require us to search for a light with a power that we think we do not have. But we have it, Harry. That's the wonder of Rabbit."

"The wonder of Rabbit?" Harry said.

"We think he's not in the hat. But he is. Put your hand into the dark of the hat; search with your fingers, and you will find him there. He is the light wrapped inside the darkness, and he is everywhere."

101

102

THE BELLS OF DARKNESS

Later that day over dinner, even Honey thought her brother looked tired.

"Are you sneaking out of the house, Brother? You look a mess. Maybe you should stop playing with my socks and get some sleep." she said.

"I am not playing with your socks. Stop." Harry said. "I'm just not sleeping so great. Pass the salad, please, Mom."

Mom set the salad bowl in front of Harry. "What is it, son? School troubles?"

"No," Harry said.

"Girl troubles?" Dad said.

104

"Absolutely not," Honey chortled.

"It's Harry's personal business," Mary said.

Harry could feel her looking at him. Sometimes his mom had the same look Samson could get. She understood Harry's gift in ways his dad and Honey didn't. He wanted to tell her about the spooky socks and the darkness twisting but he couldn't, not in front of everyone else—especially Harvest.

"Maybe you should hit the hay early tonight," Mary said.

"I might just do that." Harry finished his salad and excused himself from the table.

After his homework and one TV show, Harry climbed into his bed, totally exhausted. He drifted off quickly, but the second the clock in the foyer had chimed eleven, he awakened. Those bells from the grandfather clock were unnerving him as sure as that Edgar Allan Poe poem in American lit.

Harry wondered about the truth of the folklore about the "witching hour." He had meant to ask Samson whether or not there was any truth to the legend.

From a practical perspective, Harry understood that it was easier to do dastardly deeds in the dark. The deed could be hidden in the shadows. The illusionist was able to perform the "sleight of hand" or the "one arm vanish" with more finesse when the light was dim.

Also in American lit, Harry had recently read *The Scarlet Letter* by Nathaniel

Hawthorne. Hawthorne was buried in the Sleepy Hollow Cemetery. He wrote of the "noise of witches; who, at that period, were often heard to pass over the settlements or lonely cottages" in the height of the night between "the hour of midnight and one."

The weird dancing of those orange-and black-striped stockings certainly seemed like a nightmare to Harry. It was the aftermath of the dark-dreaming that would plague Harry in the morning. For in the harsh daylight when he awoke, there would lay once again Honey's stockings and Great-Aunt Debbie's Christmas sock.

If Harry was only experiencing nightmares, why were those socks real?

With his hands cupped behind his head, Harry did what most kids at that age do, he stared at the ceiling, wondering, trying to sleep. He wanted to hear what the voices meant when they said, "You have it wrong about 'do no evil.'" So Harry would not forget anything, he wore his "Do No Evil" T-shirt to bed along with a pair of gray sweatpants.

The grandfather clock chimed the twelve bells of midnight. Harry cringed as the last bell chimed twelve.

He looked quickly around the room, expecting to see socks or fingers. Suddenly, the many gloved fingers of the hand beneath the bed rose forming a dark fence around the bed. The closet crashed open and out of the abyss came the dancing stockings. This time, the thin and gnarled legs within the stockings gamboled across the floor as if on a quest.

The words from the poem pounded in Harry's head so loudly, he was not sure of the source of the drumming—his mind or the supernaturalness of this magic circumstance.

Oh, the bells, bells, bells!
How they clang, and clash, and roar!
What a horror they outpour...
By the twanging
And the clanging...
In the jangling

And the wrangling...
To the moaning and the groaning...
Of the bells, bells, bells!

The strange, striped stockings pranced to the edge of Harry's mattress. In a forceful jerk, the gnarled right leg kicked open the fence of gloved fingers. The gate of gloved fingers swung open in the kick, slamming against the fingers.

"The darkness awaits you with the answer!" said the voice in the dark atmosphere.

Harry sat straight up. "What do you have for me?"

The stockings danced around him and arrived at his back. The right leg kicked him. The force sent him flying off the bed, through the gate of gloved fingers, to the lurid sea of congealing, countless socks. As he looked up from the dim waves, he floated toward the open closet where the disembodied, stockinged, legs now stood at the wooden door, holding the closet open.

"Sarah Good, Sarah Good," the waves sang as Harry attempted to swim against the current of darkness. But the black-pitch tide was too strong. Harry could not resist and was through the threshold to the closet as fast as you could say "haunted house."

"Sarah Good, Sarah Good—she did all a good witch could!"

"Who are you?" Harry asked. "What do you have for me?"

He floated in the dark waves of his closet which seemed to have no end. There was no horizon, no sky, and no earth. As he looked behind him, he saw his moonlit bedroom, growing smaller and smaller, receding from his gaze.

110

"Where am I?" Harry asked of the gloom.

"Why, Harry Moon, you are in my knitting room," said the voice. The voice had changed. It was sweet and soft like the lullaby voice in a television commercial.

"Who are you?" Harry asked as he floated in the dark wool of socks.

"I thought you knew. I live inside the wood of the Sleepy Hollow Halloween Board."

Harry gasped. "I knew it. I knew that board had something to do with this. But how?" he asked the dark.

"I live inside the wood," the voice repeated.

"You live inside the wood?" Harry asked. "But why? How?"

"I was the first to be sent from the earth when they accused me of evil. They called me bad things; some called me a witch. So, I came into the wood. I refused to leave the earth. When the others were sent away, they came with me to live in the wood."

"That's Impossible," Harry said.

But the voice was unrelenting.

"Now every board that Is made at the factory on Folly Farm has a little bit of me or my others inside."

As Harry floated in the darkness, which seemed to have no end or beginning, as black as a starless, moonless night, he saw a dark figure emerge.

"Are you Sarah Good?" Harry asked.

"I am," she said.

Harry observed Sarah Good holding two knitting needles in her cloaked hands. The needles flashed in the darkness, moving so rapidly their thin, rod-like form was barely discernable. And what she was knitting seemed to be endless and unknown.

"What are you doing, Sarah Good?" Harry Moon asked the witch on her throne.

"I am knitting magic cloaks."

"Magic cloaks?" Harry asked. He was at the foot of her throne, looking up at her dark, ambiguous features hidden in the endless shadows of her hooded cowl.

"Cloaks made with darkness," she said with

a deep, gloomy sigh.

"What does the darkness want?" Harry asked.

"The world," she said. "That is why I have to tell you the truth, Harry."

"What is the truth?"

"What the world needs, Harry Moon. That's why I came to your door through the Halloween Board. You hold the wrong truth. It is not, 'DO NO EVIL.' That is where you have it wrong."

"What? How? I don't understand, Sarah," Harry said.

While Sarah Good spoke, Harry felt tiny pitter-pats moving gently across his stomach, chest, and arms. In the murky gloom, he looked at his T-shirt. Something was crawling over him, and it felt like the tiny legs of caterpillars.

113

"You have magic, boy. You can lead armies of darkness."

"My magic does not come from the Darkness, Witch Queen. My magic comes from a different place. The Great Magician looks everywhere for those to whom he can give a Rabbit. He loves the light and told me not to be afraid of the dark," Harry said.

"You are a fool!" exclaimed the queen.

114

"Rabbit is even here right now," Harry said. "He is ready to guide hearts to courage, patience, love, kindness, and *goodness*, Miss Sarah *Good*."

"I am here to tell you that the secret is not 'DO NO EVIL,' Harry Moon. It is 'DO YOU *KNOW* EVIL?'"

"Ah, the dark twisting that Samson Dupree spoke of," Harry said. "Darkness mixes the lie with the truth to create confusion and chaos for us humans, so they might lose their way. Shame on you. Life is hard enough without having to deal with silly beings like you."

"There is no path through darkness; there is no light. In this world, there are too many mansions. Harry Moon, there is no way! You struggle daily with us, Harry. Instead, join us! DO YOU KNOW EVIL? Not well enough to be effective. YOU MUST KNOW EVIL, HARRY!"

Sarah's hands seemed to fly as they worked on her knitting. "What we could do together with your magic and mine! I have mountains of cloaks ready to be worn. I have taken the wool and cotton of the lost, stray socks of civilization. I have made them ours, Harry Moon. With our magic, soon our Prince of Air will plunge the world into the darkness it so yearns for, Harry."

Harry felt the dream of dark upon him.

He could not see or feel the light.

There was only darkness.

With his mind and heart, Harry called out

to Rabbit. But there was no voice, no ripple of fur. He could feel only a stirring. He groped at the tiny thread within him. He tugged on the thread again and again, as thin and slender as it was, he could still feel it and follow it away from the dreary creature, Sarah Good. In the endless shadows, he walked and walked, pulling on the unseen thread.

This time Harry awoke to the grandfather clock chiming six. The morning sun was slanting through the room. He looked around. He was on the floor. The closet door was wide open. His chest and stomach felt scratchy. As he sat up, he noticed that he was wearing his gray sweatpants, but he was bare-chested.

His "DO NO EVIL" tee shirt in navy blue and silver glow-in-the-dark phosphorescent letters was gone. Running across his floor was a tiny, blue thread that led to the closet. As he stood, he noticed the tiny thread on the carpet moved with him. He opened his right fist and discovered a tiny, thin thread.

He followed the line of the thread from his

hand to the floor. He traced it across the floor, where he saw that the thread carried the shimmer of silvery phosphorescence. The thread led him through the closet and stopped at the back wall of the closet. It went on beyond the wall, but Harry could see no farther.

The tension in Harry's shoulders eased. He realized that this was the thread of his "DO NO EVIL" shirt that had led him back to his house.

117

Harry stood for a few seconds trying to ease his heart and mind.

It was over.

At least for now. He knew it would be best to act normal like nothing was happening. So after a cool shower, he dressed for school just like always.

But when he entered the kitchen, he saw that the Moon household was out of sorts.

Almost chaotic.

His dad was grumpy.

His mom's car would not start so she had to get a ride from Harry's dad, and for some reason, he felt upset about it.

Harvest had gotten into the box of Cheerios. Making believe they were confetti, Harvest had flung them throughout the normally orderly dining room. Mrs. Wilcox, the nanny, was busy tidying up with broom and dustbin.

Honey seemed distracted. As it was spirit day at grade school, she wore her orange-and black-tights. The stripes did not run in a straight line. They ran in squiggles.

"Look what you have done, Harry Moon!" Honey cried.

Harry thought Honey was right. All of this was his fault. Ever since his friend and enemy, Titus Kligore, had delivered the Sleepy Hollow Halloween Board to the house, there had been chaos. Nothing was normal in the Moon home. Things seemed to be falling apart at the edges.

Harry ran into the dining room. He pulled open the breakfront and took the Halloween Board from the shelf and put it under his arm. "This has to go." Then Harry grabbed his backpack and hurried to the garage with the Halloween Board. He threw open the garage door and tossed the Halloween Board onto the highest shelf and left. He would have to find a way to discard the game permanently, but for now, he felt reasonably certain that with the board out of his house, things would get back to normal.

119

"Now," Harry said. "No more knitting rooms and no more missing socks!"

Harry walked down the sidewalk toward the middle school. He strolled quickly as he was late. Ahead of him was a girl in a ponytail. She was wearing the striped stockings. On the other side of the road was a girl with chestnut hair. She, too, was wearing the orange-and-black striped stockings. As he crossed the intersection of Division Street and Aurora Street, there was a whole group of girls. They skipped, walked, and leaped as they were escorted across the street by the safety guard. The safety guard was also wearing the orange-and-black striped socks.

"This is weird," Harry said.

Everywhere he looked he saw the socks. But, what did he expect? He knew it was spirit day at the elementary school. Still, that did not keep him from being freaked out.

As he reached Maple Street, Harry Moon met up with his friend, Hao Jones.

"Is it contagious?" Hao asked, clamping his hand over his mouth.

"What?" Harry said as he continued to walk.

Hao fell into step with him. "Whatever you got," Hao mumbled under his hand. "You look terrible."

Harry stopped walking. "I know it sounds impossible, but there is a dark space where terrible creatures lurk," Harry said. "And it's in my closet."

"Who doesn't?" said Hao. "Everyone thinks that there are monsters in their closet at some time or other."

"But I met one last night during the witching hour," Harry said.

121

Hao gave Harry a shove. "Seriously, Dude. Who was it? Were you scared? I would have freaked out."

"Sarah Good," Harry said. He started walking again.

"Wow! She was the first to go. She was supposed to be a really evil woman! That's why they called her a witch and got rid of her. What was she doing in there?"

"She was knitting. Knitting dark magic cloaks for her dark army so they could walk the earth without us noticing them. And you know what she was using to make the cloaks?"

Hao tapped his chin like he was Albert Einstein or something. "Not lost socks?"

"You bet!" Harry said as they crossed the street. "That's where everyone's socks go. She takes them all for the cloaks."

"No way!"

"Way!" Harry replied.

"Wow! So that is where socks go."

"At least that's where our socks go. Into the evil knitting room of a Salem bad girl, Sarah Good."

"Bro, your stories make Sarah Good sound more and more scary."

"Sarah Good is not good, dude."

"But you know what time it is?" asked Hao.

Harry looked at his cell phone.

"Two minutes to eight," Harry said.

"It's time the Good Mischief Team cracked open the Vanquish Kit," replied Hao.

"I already took care of it. I put the Halloween Board in the garage," Harry said.

This time Hao stopped dead in his tracks. "That may not be good enough against darkness this dark."

123

124

RABBIT IN A CARREL

It was third period, and Harry had gotten a pass to go to the library. He preferred going to the library rather than study hall because it was quieter. Quiet was what he needed. Rabbit had once told him, "Sometimes, Harry, you really do have to turn it all off—the cell phone, the Xbox, the laptop, the boob-tube. You need to be with your thoughts and your Rabbit."

"Will a library carrel do?"

"That will do," Rabbit had told him. "All you need is a lonely place. A place with no interruptions."

126

Harry sat at the carrel in the far right corner of the library. He was working on an earth science term paper that was due in a few days. And lately, with all the chaos and confusion and dark twisting going on, he had little time to work on it.

It was not long before Rabbit arrived. He took a seat on the shelf of the corner cubby inside the carrel.

"Hi Rabbit," Harry said. "I'm really glad to see you."

"Hi Harry," Rabbit said. He was a bit big for the carrel. As he was deep magic, Rabbit shrunk himself down by half to accommodate

the tiny space. "I was wondering when you would find me."

"I got some help from Samson. He told me if I could not see or hear amidst the darkness, I should feel for you. You were no more than a thread last night, but I was able to pull myself through. Thanks."

"Good thing you were wearing that piece of armor," Rabbit said. His eyes crinkled, and his nose and his mouth curved upward in a little grin.

"I didn't know armor came in cotton," Harry said.

"Well, that T-shirt does have some mighty words on it. Hey, we should always use good for further good, however it comes."

"Sarah Good did not seem to like those words. She covered them up quickly," Harry said.

"You did fine," Rabbit said. "Samson was right to warn you about the dark twist. Evil loves twisting the truth around. Why do you think so many humans do it?"

"Yeah," Harry said. "It's pretty scary stuff."

"But Hao is right. It's not enough to put the Halloween Board away, for the darkness is already spreading."

"So what we have now is a case of haunted house?" Harry said as he chewed on the pencil eraser.

"That is one way of putting it," Rabbit said.

"What do we do? How do I deal with a haunted house?"

"It needs to see who's the boss. When it is clear that you are not afraid of the dark, it will *scram* as you like to say."

"I guess that doesn't mean showing them a photo of Mom and Dad?"

129

"That would be good, but that would not be best."

"So let me get this straight...Hao finally gets to open that dumb Vanquish box?"

"Such wars are not fought by flesh and blood," answered Rabbit.

"That's true, Rabbit," Harry said as he gnawed on the eraser.

"It might be time for a sleepover with the Good Mischief Team," Rabbit said.

Harry looked at Rabbit. He was a Harlequin lop-eared, or at least, that is how he presented himself. Rabbit's fur was both black and white. His face looked as if an ink bottle had exploded on it. Harry and Rabbit had been through much together. *This is my counselor, my buddy*, Harry thought.

130 The bell for fourth period rang.

"Do you know I love you, Rabbit?" said Harry.

"Oh, you're just saying that because I got you all excited about the idea of another sleepover," said Rabbit.

"Not only for that," said Harry, as he put his notebook in his backpack. "But for all you do for me." Harry slung his backpack over his shoulders.

"I do it because of love," said Rabbit. "Because I love you, Harry Moon. You know where to find me. I'm right there inside you."

Harry checked the surface of the desk on the carrel to see if he had left anything behind. He took his pencil and crammed it into the left pocket of his jeans.

"A sleepover," Harry said. "We'll figure this out."

132

PREPARING FOR WAR

Lunch time could not come soon enough for Harry. He had to talk to the Good Mischief Team about the sleepover and, of course, the spooky socks situation.

"Listen, you guys, it's time to wage war against the socks."

"We're in," Bailey said with gusto.

"Time for the vanquishing kit," Hao said.

"But listen, we can't just do it. We have to plan, so I want you guys to come to my house for a sleepover tonight."

"Sure," the guys said.

"Great, check with your moms, first." And speaking of which, Harry had yet to ask his mom if it would be all right with her.

134

"It's okay with you, then?" Harry said into his cell.

"Yes, as long as the boys' parents agree," Mary Moon said. "Is everything alright, Harry? You sound a little worried."

"Samson helped me figure it all out, Mom. I'm cool."

Harry nodded his head to the guys at the table. They raised their hands and high-fived each other.

"Well," Mom said. "Mrs. Wilcox said you took that Halloween Board out of the breakfront and moved it to the garage."

"I did, Mom. But, everything is fine, really. Or it will be fine."

"Make sure that Bailey does not bring cherry bombs upstairs. I want no more cherry bombs in the house. Am I clear with you on that, Harry?"

"Yes, Mom. Thanks, Mom. Bye, Mom."

"Good-bye, Harry, I love you."

"I love you, too, Mom," Harry said. He clicked the phone off.

"Party tonight!" Declan said.

""I'll bring a barrel of Cheetos and a large assortment of Little Debbie snacks," announced the foodie, Hao.

"This is not all fun and video games. We

have serious work to do," Harry said.

"Right," Bailey said. "We know, but there's nothing wrong with mixing fun with work. Work makes me hungry."

"Everything makes you hungry," Harry said. "I'll get my dad to make us his famous late-night cheeseburgers."

"You mean before the *witching hour*? Or after the *witching hour*?" asked Bailey enthusiastically, his eyes full of relish and delight.

"Before," said Harry, "we'll need our strength. And maybe after too, to celebrate our victory!"

"To victory!" cheered the Good Mischief Team.

"But no cherry bombs, Bailey. My mom was adamant," Harry said.

"Okay, okay," Bailey said as he lowered his eyes. "I paid for the new toilet, didn't I?"

Harry looked over at his friend. He patted Bailey on the back. "My mom just doesn't want you have to pay for another one, that's all."

"Besides, we don't need bombs or guns," Declan said. "This is a war fought not with flesh and blood but with your Rabbit buddy, right?"

"Right!" Hao cheered, excited to finally be using his vanquishing kit.

"Nothing is going to go wrong, for we are in the right! Right?" Bailey asked, confidently.

"Right!" the guys answered with another cheer.

That was when Mrs. Reynolds told them to quiet down.

The Good Mischief Team had settled into Harry Moon's bedroom with snacks and sleeping bags. It was not the first time for a sleepover, and if the guys placed their sleeping bags not in a row but more like a quilt, four friends in one room worked out just fine. They all wore their "DO NO EVIL" t-shirts.

It was a warm, fall night. It was one of those comfortable, clear nights just made for barbecue. True to his word, for he was always a dad of his word, John Moon was grilling cheese-burgers in the backyard. The smell drifting up through the open window was unbelievable. It was around eleven o'clock, a good hour before the witching hour. The white smoke from the grill was pouring into the sky as John Moon put the final touches on the burgers—Swiss cheese. Mr. Moon was giving advice to Harry and his friends and making sure they were going to handle the vanquishing correctly.

"Boys, you have to test the spirits," Dad said as he put the top on the grill for just one minute so the cheese would melt just right.

"How do we do that, Mr. Moon?" asked Hao.

"Well, the spirits are either with you or against you. They are either with what's good and right or they are against it, understand?"

"I know for sure, they are against it!" said Harry as he passed out the paper plates to everyone.

"Be careful," said Harry's dad. "Always remember that the darkness wants to convince you that it is good."

Harry and the Good Mischief Team listened as they sat at the picnic table.

"Geeze," Bailey said, "this is as good as any old, spooky campfire story."

"Better," Harry said. "Because it's true."

Dad lifted the BBQ lid. "Ahhh, almost there. Five more seconds will do it."

140

Hao inhaled deeply and then let it out through his nose like a bull. "But what do we do? How do we test spirits?"

Bailey said, "I got some holy water from the Catholic church."

"Yeah, we put it in the vanquishing kit," Hao said. "And when they come at us, Mr. Moon, we will throw it at 'em and watch them disintegrate, right?"

"That may only be in the movies," John Moon said. He smiled as he lifted the top off the grill. "Ahhhhh, burger perfection."

Smoke poured into the sky while he took each cheeseburger off the grill with his spatula and laid it on a waiting bun on the guys' plates.

"It's in a lot of movies," Harry said.

"Okay, but in real life, what do we do?" asked Declan.

The guys dug into their food.

141

"It's pretty simple," John Moon answered. "You just have to speak into the darkness, 'Are you good?' There are three ways they will answer. Yes, is the only answer that you want to hear. Obviously 'no' means that they are with the army of darkness."

"And what is the third answer?" asked Harry.

"They do not answer at all. They will change the subject, avoid the question, or not say anything," John Moon said as he squeezed an extra helping of ketchup on his burger patty. "They are the most dangerous."

"Where did you learn that, Mr. Moon? Was that in the original Ghostbusters?" asked Bailey with a mouthful of burger.

"Let's just say that when I was growing up, my grandmother and I had to take care of some trouble in the barn when we lived in Gloucester," Harry's dad said. "We learned the hard way. But we learned. Just take that silver-rimmed mirror out and compel them to leave by putting it in front of their face."

"But vampires don't have any reflections," Harry said.

"Right," Hao said. "That's just it. Not having a reflection freaks them out and it snaps them out of their delusion, and they can know the truth."

"Wow," Declan said. "I guess if I looked into a mirror and only saw darkness and blackness it would freak me out too."

"Yeah, it would," Hao said. "No reflection. Imagine that."

As the boys looked at one another across the picnic table, the phosphorescence from their shirts shone in the moonlight.

144

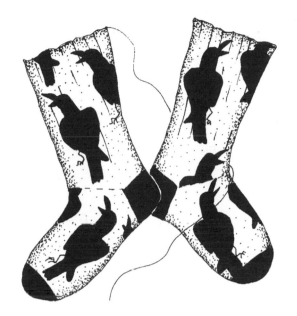

GOOD MISCHIEF

Harry watched his alarm clock turn to 11:39 when they got back to his room. They had piled their sleeping bags in the far right corner of the room, away from the closet. Harry's steamer trunk with the painted moons had been pushed to the corner as well. If the war got rough, the Good Mischief Team wanted plenty of room to vanquish.

Hao looked around the room. "I kind of feel like we are living inside a ghost story."

There was a knock at the door just as Hao said that, and they all jumped.

"Oh, Mom," Harry said. "You kind of scared us."

"Oh, I'm sorry, dear. I didn't mean to. Just brought some water bottles."

"Hey, Mrs. Moon," Bailey said. "I did just as Harry promised you. No cherry bombs."

"Thank you, Bailey. I brought you all waters in case you get thirsty. You all know where the bathroom is. And remember, lights out at one. I'll have breakfast ready for you at nine downstairs, so you can all get your eight hours sleep."

The boys each took their bottles of water and thanked Harry's mom for her hospitality.

Once his mom left the room, Harry went to

the door and locked it.

"Why'd you do that?" asked Declan, his voice quivering.

"We don't want the darkness spreading any farther than this room," Harry said.

"Do you think a locked door is going to seal it in?" asked Declan.

"It slows it down," Harry replied. "C'mon, let's get a closer look at the vanquishing kit."

147

Hao had set the kit on Harry's bed. It was an old, brown, leather attaché case with a brass latch. Hao Jones's dad had purchased the ancient briefcase in a yard sale in Connecticut. It was said to have been used in the Civil War era. There were some old newspaper clippings about President Abraham Lincoln at the bottom of the case to attest to that story.

Reverently, Hao opened the leather case.

The case was lined with black velvet. The objects for the vanquishing were embedded in sewn pockets of velvet—there was a small glass jar with a silver lid for holy water, which Bailey had already procured from the church. There was a packet of old religious cards, which were so ancient that they crackled with age as you touched them. There were several sterling silver mirrors which Hao handed to each of the guys.

"What's that?" Bailey asked. He pointed at a small, glass bottle.

"Garlic powder," Hao said. "Vampires hate garlic."

"But we're fighting the evil in the darkness," Bailey said.

Harry took the garlic powder out of the case and examined it. "Same kind of thing. It's the evil we're after, not the body they choose to inhabit."

"Ohhhhhh," Bailey said. "That makes sense."

Harry pulled another bottle from the case. "Vampire Dust," he read.

"Yeah," Hao said. "This evil stuff gets really tough. It does not go down easy unless you sprinkle vampire dust on it. It really messes up the mojo."

"Mojo?" Harry said. "I think you mean their essence."

"Whatever," Hao said. "Vampire dust makes them more vulnerable to the light—I think."

149

From one of the velvet pockets, Hao pulled four pen flashlights. He handed one to each boy and kept one for himself, slipping it into his pocket.

Holding the mirrors in their right hands, the boys brought both hands together in a huddle.

"Harry, will you do the honors?" asked Declan. "After all, you are the magician on the team."

Harry thought for a moment. As he had learned from Rabbit, he took a deep breath and collected all of himself—his mind, heart, body, and soul—under all the wisdom he had learned from his furry friend. He spoke softly but with strength.

"Listen up, guys," Harry said. "Good is good and evil is evil. There's nothing in between here. No gray areas. If the darkness says it is against good, hold up your mirror. Got it?"

150

"Yeah," the guys said.

"The socks are just a ruse. We're after the true evil that lives in the abyss."

Harry could feel Bailey shaking next to him. "Listen, dude," Harry said. "If you're too scared, it's okay. You can take off."

"No, no," Bailey said. "I'm not scared. No more than all of you."

"Yeah," Hao said. "One for all and all for one."

"Let's torch the darkness," Harry said.

Harry walked toward the closet. He picked up the tiny blue thread to his original "DO NO EVIL" tee shirt that had unraveled the previous night. He knew the thread would be the tiny and singular road that would guide the Good Mischief Team. The team would pass through the closet wall and into the heart of darkness where Sarah Good conducted her knitting. Together they would enter that supernatural room where those knitting needles flashed with the energy of evil deeds

151

."You have the thread?" Hao asked.

"Got it," said Harry, holding the thread tight. Harry walked over to the light switch by the door and flicked it off. The ceiling light went dim. It was now completely dark.

"Hey, why'd you do that?" asked Declan, his voice quivering again.

"So we can get used to the dark," Harry replied.

"It's ten to midnight," said Declan, "Do we need a whole ten minutes to get used to the dark?"

"I don't know," said Harry. "Let's do five minutes then."

He flicked the ceiling light back on. They stood in the light, silently, not sure what to do. It was neither time for Cheetos nor time to check out their cell phones. Indeed, it was time for the witching hour. They waited, watching one another, their mirrors in their right hands.

Harry had tucked the bottle of garlic powder in his pocket just in case. And he had taken the vampire dust also. Best to be prepared.

"Remember, these spirits could be under a spell," Harry whispered. "When they see the mirrors, they might shriek or moan. Don't be afraid. It's because they are in shock, dealing with the deceit in which they have been living. Ignore their shrieking and noise."

"Wow, where'd you get that?" asked Hao, impressed. "I always wondered why those vampires screamed in the movies."

153

"I got it from Rabbit. He not only knows. Rabbit understands."

Harry looked at his alarm clock. He squeezed the blue thread tightly in his hand. When the clock flipped to 11:58 Harry flicked off the light, plunging the room, once again, into the dark.

"It doesn't take long at all," said Declan, his voice quivering in the black, "to get used to the dark."

In the shadowy, murky room, the boys could hear themselves breathing. That is until the bells from the first floor chimed twelve times.

The witching hour was upon them.

Midnight had arrived.

The closet door crashed open with a thunderous roar.

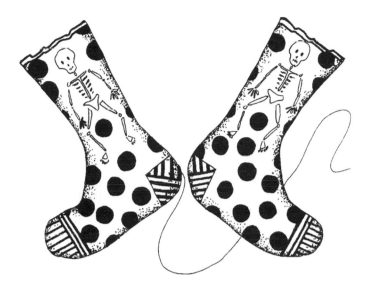

THE WITCHING HOUR

T he gloomy silhouette of the orange-and-black, striped stockings stepped out of the closet through the open door. Lost socks rose from beneath Harry's bed and floated into the dark atmosphere of the room. As the socks crept upward, the boys could feel the scratch of wool and cotton and frayed threads moving over their bodies and bare faces. Declan was so frightened that he almost peed his pants—

but he didn't. After all, Declan was part of the Good Mischief Team. They did not soak their clothes.

"Oh, ouch!" Declan said. "The darkness is heavy. I feel it, Harry!"

"Hold on to my shirt," Harry said. "We now have access into the darkness. All of you hold on to my shirt. I'll walk slowly and lead us in by the thread."

The guys stayed as close to each other as they could and moved along the closet wall. The room grew deeper and darker with each nervous step.

Declan yanked on a fistful of cotton.

"Harry, is that you?" Declan asked.

"Still me, hold on tight," Harry said. "C'mon, guys, just as we planned. Stay close. We go together."

Bailey searched and found a hunk of shirt

at Harry's back to grab as well.

"Harry, Is that you?" said Bailey as he tugged on the dark cloth.

"Still me," reassured Harry.

Now with two of the guys holding on to Harry's "DO NO EVIL" shirt, Harry waited for Hao.

"Harry, is that you?" said Hao as he pulled at the fabric.

"No, it is not!" said Harry.

"Then what am I holding onto?" asked Hao as he pulled on the cloth again.

"I dunno; it is not me," Harry said.

"It is me, you fools!" said another voice. "Sarah Good!"

Harry stopped dead in his tracks, which made the others crash into him like a train wreck.

"Sarah Good!" Hao shouted.

"Yes, you darling fool," Sarah said. "You have gotten a hold of the robe and cloak I am knitting you, Hao Jones! Hang on tight."

"What?" cried Hao.

"Who needs Harry's little thread when you can be with me now!" Sarah Good said. Then she let out a cackling laugh.

"Hao, I'm over here," Harry said.

"Hao, are you there?" said Bailey, holding on for dear life to Harry's shirt.

"Come closer, Hao," Declan said in his quivering voice.

In the darkness, there was no sound of Hao.

"Hao?" Harry called out. "Hao!"

Still, there was no response.

"I guess he took the expressway in," said Bailey.

Harry grabbed the thread and slowly pulled on it. Step by step, Harry, his two friends holding the back of his shirt, moved deeper into the closet. They went deeper and deeper into the dark murk. Soon, they walked past, or through, the back wall.

159

There was silence in the pitch black for several minutes.

Then, like distant waves crashing on the shoreline, a soft, low drum of sound began to pound. The noise was low and vibrated at the boys' feet. As Harry tugged on the thread, he and the other boys approached the deep darkness of the house. There was the whip of wings flying, the patter of rain splattering, and the rumble of thunder that rolled but did not clap.

"DOYOUKNOWEVIL?" the sound rumbled.

"Don't listen to that!" said Harry.

"DOYOUKNOWEVIL?" the darkness asked.

"Do no evil!" Harry shouted back. "Do no evil!"

"OOOOOH," cried the clamoring darkness. Y O U K N O W E V I L, B U T Y O U W A N T T O K N O W M O R E?"

"C'mon, guys!" Harry cried. "Repeat it with me. "'Do no evil!'" It was so dark that the boys could see nothing. All they could do was follow Harry by clinging to his shirt and shouting with him.

"Do no evil! Do no evil!" they cried.

"Louder!" Harry shouted.

"DO NO EVIL! DO NO EVIL!" the three boys shouted. "DO NO EVIL!"

"How marvelous!" The darkness trumpeted in a big roar as loud as a wave crashing on the ocean's shore. "Come to me and learn more!"

"Do not twist our words, darkness!" Harry shouted. "Leave this house!"

"Why would we leave when we have much to teach you?"

The darkness laughed. *Bwahahahahaha-hahha.* "Let go of your Rabbit!"

As the darkness shrieked, the boys felt pressure at their backs. The waves of wool and cotton pushed at them. Their knees buckled. As they fell under the pressure, the gloom rolled over them, turning them like cloth in the tumbler of a dryer. They turned over and over again. They were rolling fast through the darkness, holding tight to the mirrors in their fists.

This was a world Harry did not know. He reached for his light. He tumbled still farther and farther. There was no ground or sky—just massive darkness, pressing and pulling, moving them forward until they reached a wall of dark, dark wool.

Black yarn scratched at their faces. Then they stopped moving.

As Harry looked up, he saw the dim silhouette of Sarah Good on her throne. They had reached the knitting room. Harry could see the flashing glint of knitting needles working above him.

"What have you done with Hao?" Harry shouted.

"Ohhhh, do not worry about your friend. He is with me. Safe and sound. He will be useful to me."

"Give us back Hao!" Harry shouted.

"He is no longer with you. He is with me now," shouted Sarah Good.

"No, he's not! We want him back!" Bailey shouted at Sarah.

"For years I and my kin hid in the wood. Now, Hao Jones hides in our wool! You shall never have him. But move farther, try to find him, if you choose, Harry Moon!"

"Light me up, guys!" Harry said.

163

The boys' penlights suddenly shone brightly in the black, black room.

"This is where the twist ends!" Harry said.

Two penlights flashed on. Their white beams bounced off the mirror in Harry's outstretched fist.

"It is, 'DO NO EVIL' TIME!" Harry shouted, pushing the mirror closer to Sarah Good's face.

For the first time, she could be seen. Her face was wan and thin, the skin tight against the shape of her skull. Her dark eyes were set deep in her face and gleamed with fury as Harry held out the mirror.

"Look!" Harry shouted. "Look for your reflection and tell me," Harry cried, "are you good?"

"Not in this world, child!" said Sarah. "There is no goodness. Darkness rules earth."

"No, you are wrong. Goodness reigns

over the universe and will extinguish your darkness."

Harry pulled the penlight from his pocket as he spoke. He shined it on the mirror that he held upright.

"You have false language, kiddo!" cried Sarah Good. She dropped her knitting needles. She grabbed the arms of her throne and stood before the Good Mischief Team. She towered over them. "You will not defeat the darkness!" she said.

"Goodness will always win!" Harry cried. When he said it, Declan and Bailey held up their mirrors. "Do no evil," they cried out into the dark. "Do no evil."

As they spoke, they created their own wall. This wall was light. For as the penlights shone upon the mirrors, the silver took on the light.

"Darkness, leave this house! Do no evil!" Harry cried.

"You cannot demand me! You cannot speak to me that way!" cried Sarah Good, her eyes flashing with crimson fire.

"My house, my rules!" Harry cried. "Now scram; by all that is good, scram!" Harry shouted.

As the three guys continued to shout, "Do no evil!" their wall of light grew even larger. In the light, they saw their friend, Hao Jones, wrapped in a cocoon of dark wool, his face peering through the fibers.

"Go get him, Bailey," Harry whispered. "Go get Hao."

Bailey lunged forward. He ripped the wool from Hao's body. Hao dropped to the ground like a sack of potatoes.

"Hao," Bailey said. He slapped his face. "Wake up, man. Wake up."

Harry saw Hao's eyes open. "Bring him back."

As Bailey helped Hao stand, Harry felt strength and courage surge through his body. He had passed through the fear and into courage.

Harry gripped the mirror and thrust it toward Sarah.

"Look at it," Harry called. "Find your true self in this mirror."

"Never. You cannot make me." Sarah shrieked.

Harry reached for the bottle of vampire dust. He pulled out the cork and dropped it to the floor. Then he threw the strange, glowing gray ashes at Sarah. "How about a little vampire dust, Witch!"

"Nooooo," she cried. "Don't."

"Look," Harry called. "See yourself for who you really are."

Harry watched as Sarah's eyes peered into

the mirror. "Don't make me see. Don't make me see." Then she let out an ear-piercing shriek that shook Harry to his core, yet he stood strong, planted in the truth.

Then Sarah Good began to grow smaller and smaller. While her throne remained large, she continued to dwindle, not able to speak or move by the power of goodness. The great, dark, shapeless sea that had once surrounded them began to reveal itself. Instead of the overwhelming darkness, thousands and thousands of socks that had once comprised the waves, which had rolled the Good Mischief Team to the feet of the witch, took form. The supernatural knitting room was, literally, unraveling under the truth revealed inside the mirrors.

"Get it, Sarah?" Harry called. "It's DO NO EVIL, WITCH!"

As he shouted, Sarah dwindled. She grew so tiny that she could no longer be seen on her throne. The waves of the dark sea broke apart, and the four guys fell through it.

They dropped onto the floor of Harry's room, along with dozens of stray socks, all in dark colors. Harry and the Good Mischief Team were sitting on a pile of socks. The moonlight slanted through the bedroom window, shining on the phosphorescent letters emblazoned across their shirts.

The hallway door crashed open.

"Hey, I locked that door!" Harry said.

Honey flicked on the light in the room. In her arms were dozens of socks.

"Look!" she said. "They fell out from nowhere onto my bed! What's going on in here?"

"Don't be scared," Harry said. "They can't hurt us anymore."

She opened her arms and dropped the pile of socks onto the floor. "There's even my dance sock from first grade in this pile!" she said as she picked up a pink heel sock from the floor and showed it to Harry and his friends.

The guys looked at Honey and then at the other socks scattered across the carpeted floor.

"Oh, Harry, this is all my fault!" Honey said.

"All your fault?"

"Yes, I opened the Halloween Board. I wanted to see if it really worked, if it really was magical," Honey said.

"Oh, that's what happened," Hao said. "Not a good idea."

"I wish Titus never brought that stupid Board into our house," Honey said.

Harry climbed out of the pile of socks. "It wasn't even really Titus's fault," Harry said.

"It was his father's idea," Declan said.

Honey added her armful of socks to the now not spooky socks.

"Hey," called Harry's dad. "What gives?" He was standing at the door holding several pairs of Argyle socks. "These fell on top of me."

"Sorry, Dad," Harry said.

"I take it your vanquishing act was a success?" Dad said.

"It sure was, Dad," Harry said.

"Nice to have my socks back," Dad said. "I've always wondered what happened to all the socks that go missing, and now we know, I suppose."

"They were hidden in the dark!" cried Honey.

That was when Harry's mother arrived carrying a bundle of miscellaneous socks from toddler size to adult. She even carried Christmas socks and striped socks and even several pairs of heavy, wool hunting socks.

"Hey, Mom," Harry said. "Find some socks?"

"What is this about, Harry?"

The rising sun shone through the window blinds. Harry's stomach rumbled. "It's a long story, Mom," he said.

"Well, I want to hear all about it," Mom said. "How about you tell me over a nice breakfast."

"You bet," Declan said. "We worked up quite an appetite. Lighting the dark is hard work."

"Okay," Mom said. "I'll make a nice breakfast. You can tell me over pancakes."

"I'll take care of Harvest," John Moon said.

After his parents and Honey left, Harry went to the closet. Back to normal. No darkness. Just his clothes—back to normal.

"We did it," Harry said. "You guys are the best."

They high-fived each other and then tossed socks around in a more playful sock battle.

⌒ᔑ⌐

Breakfast looked amazing. Harry's mom set out a great spread. She made pancakes and sausage. But there was also plenty of fresh fruit and even a fruit smoothie.

"So, nothing to worry about, Mom," said Harry as he picked up a forkful of hot pancake.

Everyone sat around the table. Harvest smeared blueberry syrup on his high chair tray. Honey did her best to keep him clean until John Moon finally intervened.

173

"It's all right. A little blueberry syrup in his hair won't hurt."

"Tell me the whole story," Mom said.

With help from the Team, Harry told his mother everything that had happened. When he had finished, John Moon said, "Peace has returned to the kingdom." He beamed, obviously proud of Harry and the Good

Mischief Team.

The boys and the Moons all held up their smoothies and toasted to peace and goodness. Harry glanced at the dining room wall, at the words that surrounded them. He felt comforted and happy.

"I think it's best if it stays this way," Mom said. She poured old-fashioned maple syrup over her pancakes.

"What do you mean?" Harry asked.

"Where is that Halloween Board?" asked Mary Moon. "I think it's about to have a date with destiny."

"What are you going to do, Mom?" asked Honey.

"Well, as pretty as it is, I think it must be destroyed."

"Good idea, Mom," Harry said. "I'll cut it into tiny pieces after breakfast."

John Moon chewed and swallowed. "No, no, that will not do. The board must be burned. Set fire to it."

"Of course," Harry said. "The darkness can still live in the wood otherwise."

"Exactly," Dad said. "We'll burn it to ashes."

175

176

GRILLED CORN AND
A BURNING BOARD

H arry did not burn the board immediately. It wasn't until later that day that he was able to muster his courage to retrieve the board from the garage. But even as he stood there with the box in his hand, the old, frightening feelings returned. He knew he was holding Sarah Good's last stronghold in his hands. He also knew the job had to be finished.

It was closing in on dinner time when Harry finally brought the board to the backyard. His Dad was just firing up the grill. The Moon's had planned a late dinner, which was fine with Harry. Dinner was best under the glow of the moon and light from the white fairy lights he had strung all around the yard.

"Oh, Harry," Dad said. "Just in time. Would you run into the house and grab the corn?"

"Sure, Dad," Harry said. He set the box on the picnic table. Then he ran into the house. He was standing in the kitchen just about to snag the corn when he heard, "Titus!"

"What?" Harry said. "Is he here again?"

Harry left the corn and went to the living room. Sure enough, Titus was standing there talking to his mother.

"Hullo, Mrs. Moon," Titus said as he nodded and smiled.

"Titus?" Harry said. "What's up?"

"I invited him, Harry," Mom said.

"Oh," Harry said. "Okay, I guess."

"Hey, Moon," Titus said. "I hope it's okay. You know, with all the trouble lately."

179

Harry felt a smile stretch across his face. "Yeah," he said. "In fact, you can help me with the fire in the fire pit. Dad thought it would be fun to have a little campfire tonight."

"Good idea, Harry," Mom said.

Titus followed Harry through the house. "Why do I have a feeling you're up to something?"

"Because we are," Harry said.

"Right," Mom said. "Now, don't get me

wrong, I appreciate the gift of the Halloween Board and all, but let's just say it's not right for our family."

Harry nudged Titus into the backyard. "Yeah, Kligore, we have to get rid of that thing in the only permanent way we can."

"How's that?" Titus asked.

"We're gonna burn it."

Harry and Titus stepped into the backyard where the aroma of grilling chicken and corn on the cob wafted through the air.

"Sorry, Dad," Harry said. "I was gonna get the corn when Titus came by."

"It's okay, Harry," Dad said.

"C'mon, c'mon," Honey hollered. "Let's get this party started."

"All right, all right," Harry called.

Harry got a small fire started in the fire pit. It was just getting going with orange flames lapping into the night sky.

"Go get the board, Titus," he said.

"It's over here," Honey called. "On the picnic table."

"Do it, Titus," Harry said. "Time you took a stand."

Titus grabbed the board. Harry's mom put her hand on Titus's shoulder. "It's the right thing to do."

Titus carried the box to Harry. "You do it, Moon. I can't."

"No," Harry said. "I think you should. Just put it on the flames. Let the fire do the job."

182

"Should I open it?" Titus asked.

Harry shook his head. "I don't think that's a good idea. Just put the whole thing on. It will burn."

Titus took a deep, deep breath and set the Sleepy Hollow Halloween Board onto the hot flames. In moments the box caught fire. Orange and purple and red flames shot into the night sky.

With his special eyes, Harry looked into the

smoke. While the game burned, Harry thought about the darkness it contained. He watched as the smoke twisted and then unfurled toward the stars.

"I hope you understand, Titus," John Moon said. "I am sorry. No offense to your family but we had to do this."

"I totally get it, Mr. M, no apologies necessary," said Titus.

183

"There's a lot of noise out there in the world, Titus. For the sake of our family, we try to keep the noise level down here at Chez Moon."

"I get it, Mr. M. Truth is, the reason I like coming over here is because it's peaceful-like."

"You know what I have learned, Titus, man-to-man?" asked John Moon.

Harry listened as the box burned.

"The only way to peace in the world is to

have peace in your heart first," John Moon said.

"I get that," Titus said. "I am learning that. I think I really am—from Harry and all of you and those great words in the dining room."

After the fire had dwindled down, everyone enjoyed chicken and corn.

"This is the best food, ever," Titus said. "I like it better than that fancy stuff my dad makes the cooks serve us."

"Well, eat up, Titus," Mom said.

The family talk was fun. For dessert, Honey served strawberry shortcake. She and Mom made it together. It was a little lopsided but tasted just fine. Titus had three servings.

After dinner, Harry Moon announced he had a special treat, courtesy of Samson Dupree.

Harry stood up from the picnic table and

put his hands at his back.

"Now, Harvest, I am relying on you. On the count of three. Are you ready?"

"Ready!" Harvest said.

"One, two..." Harry said as he looked over at his baby brother. Together they shouted, "ABRACADABRA."

Harry pulled his hands from behind his back and revealed a fistful of sparklers all lit up and sparking like mad.

"Sparklers!" Harvest cried as he jumped out of his booster chair.

Harry handed sparklers to everyone. Honey and Harvest took off running with theirs.

"No, thanks," Titus said.

"Why not?" Harry asked.

"Don't you think we're a little old for this,

bro?" Titus asked.

"Are you kidding? Just look," Harry said. Titus turned to see Mr. and Mrs. Moon running through the grass—their shining lights above them. Mr. Moon had two sparklers, one in each hand and was masquerading as a B-14 bomber.

"Well, okay, Harry," Titus said. "But mostly I don't think I deserve to join the fun."

Harry handed Titus a sparkler. "Sure you do. Everyone deserves fun and maybe a little slice of heaven from time to time."

"Heaven?" Titus said. "Now that's something I am sure I don't get."

Titus took the sparkler and smiled. "I never did this before."

"You know what Rabbit says?" Harry asked.

"What's that?" Titus asked.

"We don't need to wait for heaven. Heaven is right here," said Harry as Harvest pulled on his shirt looking for another sparkler. By simply snapping his fingers, Harry lit a fresh sparkler for his brother.

"Heaven!" said Harvest as he and Honey took the sparkler and went running off again.

Titus and Harry did not go running through the grass that night. Titus just sat on the grass in silence.

"Whatcha thinking about?" Harry asked.

"Just stuff," Titus said. "The words in your dining room, Rabbit, heaven. Just stuff."

"That's all good stuff," Harry said.

"Yeah," Titus said. "Good stuff."

188

THAT TERRIBLE PEACE AGAIN

The following Thursday, the Kligores were having their weekly family dinner night.

The cook, silver-haired Estelle Buber, served dinner from a serving tray. They ate in the great Feast Hall at the Folly Farm Estate.

Of course, it was more like a board meeting of the We Drive By Night Company then quality time between a dad and his children. Tonight, it wasn't oysters for the mayor. Tonight, it was lobster—served in the shell. Titus's dad enjoyed cracking the skin of the crustacean and tearing out the meat.

"I feel like a gladiator!" he told his children. Clarice, Titus, and Marcus listened submissively. "Wow! Do I love lobster—you gotta go to battle with it to get the good stuff!"

Titus tried to be respectful, but on that one, he had to roll his eyes. This was not lost on the mayor who, it has been said, had eyes in the back of his head.

"So, Titus, you have been awfully quiet. You need to fill me in," the mayor asked as he dipped the lobster's claw meat into a silver bowl of melted butter. "How did the Moon family like that Salem Woodburn font?"

"Oh, Mrs. Moon knew all about Sarah Good stuff and the special S."

"Oh, that woman really knows her fonts!" Maximus said.

"What special S?" asked Marcus.

"Oh, you don't know about the special S?" said Titus to his older brother. "The Salem Woodburn font had an S with a line through it indicating that you had a special thing going with darkness."

"Cool," Maximus said.

191

"It's a goofy game," said Titus.

"Hey, don't knock it," said the mayor. "Salem's Woodburn helps put lobster on this table!"

"That's why I am having vegetables," said Titus.

"You're a vegetarian?" asked Marcus.

"I am trying a few things out," Titus said.

"Don't start going sissy on us over there in middle school, Titus," said Clarice as she sucked the meat out of the lobster claw.

Staring at his brother, Marcus threw his claw shell to the floor. "You are such dweeb."

Oink was waiting for the scraps, and he chomped and slobbered on his red pile of shell scraps.

"So how did the peaceful Moon house like the Halloween Board?" asked the mayor.

"Oh, they loved it, Dad," replied Titus. "For a little while, anyway."

"What wonderful life did that Halloween Board bring to that dull, sad household? I have to check in on my happy constituency. I am mayor of Sleepy Hollow, after all."

"Well, first Harry said he just had a creepy feeling. And then these weird socks started dancing at night."

"Oh, I love it!" said the mayor, so delighted he started on his second lobster. "Tell me more, please, son! I am not sensing the chaos yet." Maximus adjusted his lobster bib.

"More like action, Dad." Titus swallowed. Hard. "Now don't get mad, Dad, but then they burned it up in a fire."

"Oh," said the mayor.

"Yeah, Harry said it was the only way to get rid of the darkness it had brought to their home."

"I think a little part of me just died," said Maximus with a sigh. He sat back in his chair.

"They burned the game? Wow," said Clarice.

"Then what happened?" asked Marcus.

"We ate dinner. Chicken and corn and salad and strawberry shortcake."

"That's it?" said Marcus as he threw some

more shells down to his garbage disposal, Oink.

"Well, first they said a dinner prayer at the picnic table, wishing all humankind peace on earth and goodwill to all."

"There's that terrible peace thing again. I hate peace!" the mayor said.

"Peace?" Marcus said. "It's just another way to say boring."

194

"It is not," Titus said. "It's kind of nice."

"Come on, Titus," Marcus said. "What am I going to say to my buds on Saturday night? 'Let's go find some peace.'"

"The Moons are into that, Dad. It's on their wall," said Titus.

"Don't start going all goodness and light on us, brother," Clarice said.

"I must confess, I am very disappointed in this outcome," said Maximus to his son. "It has almost ruined my appetite. I will have only one slice of key lime," Maximus said to Estelle as she cleared his plate of two lobster carcasses.

"There you go, Dad, you're showing some healthy restraint," said Titus.

"Estelle, make that two," Maximus called to Estelle in the kitchen.

The mayor looked across the table at his youngest son. He shook his head as if to shake a disagreeable image from his mind.

195

"What's going on?" asked the mayor.

"What?" asked Titus.

"Do you see it, Marcus?" the mayor asked.

Marcus looked over at his younger brother. He saw Titus finishing his broccoli.

"See what?"

"I thought I saw a rabbit standing next to Titus."

Titus laughed.

"Stranger things have happened," Titus replied.

The blood rose in the mayor's face. "I do not want you going over to that Moon house anymore; do you hear me, Titus?"

"Don't be mad at me, Dad," said Titus with a respectful laugh. "I did not see the rabbit; you did."

Rabbits are for all people. You simply need to ask.

197

198

MARK ANDREW POE

The Adventures of Harry Moon author Mark Andrew Poe never thought about being a children's writer growing up. His dream was to love and care for animals, specifically his friends in the rabbit community.

Along the way, Mark became successful in all sorts of interesting careers. He entered the print and publishing world as a young man and his company did really, really well.

Mark became a popular and nationally sought-after health care advocate for the care and well-being of rabbits.

Years ago, Mark came up with the idea of a story about a young man with a special connection to a world of magic, all revealed through a remarkable rabbit friend. Mark worked on his idea for several years before building a collaborative creative team

199

to help bring his idea to life. And Harry Moon was born.

In 2014, Mark began a multi-book print series project intended to launch *The Adventures of Harry Moon* into the youth marketplace as a hero defined by a love for a magic where love and 'DO NO EVIL' live. Today, Mark continues to work on the many stories of Harry Moon.   He lives in suburban Chicago with his wife and his 25 rabbits.

BE SURE TO READ THE CONTINUING AND AMAZING ADVENTURES OF HARRY MOON

THE
AMAZING
Adventures Of
HARRY MOON
Wand - Paper - Scissors

Inspired by true events   Mark Andrew Poe

THE
AMAZING
Adventures Of
HARRY MOON
Halloween Nightmares

Inspired by true events   Mark Andrew Poe

THE
AMAZING
Adventures Of
HARRY MOON
Time Machine

Inspired by true events   Mark Andrew Poe

THE
AMAZING
Adventures Of
HARRY MOON
The Scary Smart House

Inspired by true events   Mark Andrew Poe

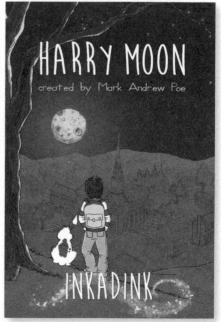

Graphic novel

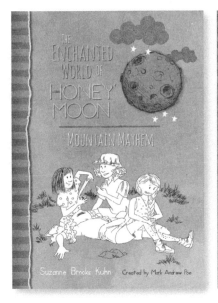